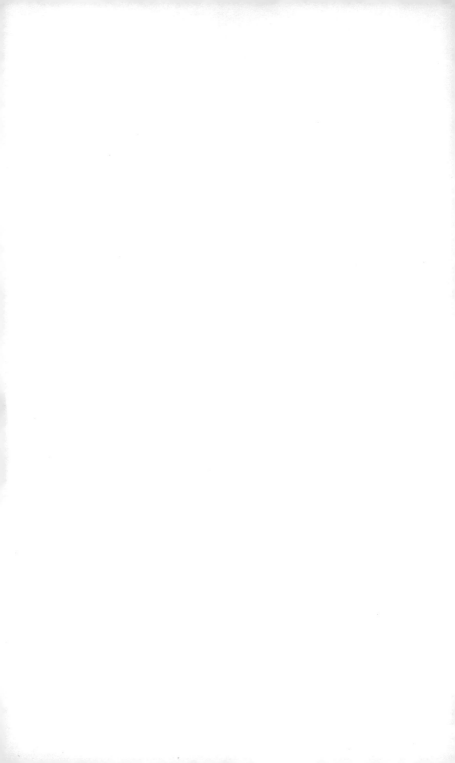

# *Turning* LEAD *into* GOLD

## THE DEMYSTIFICATION OF OUTSOURCING

PETER BENDOR-SAMUEL

**For permissions requests, contact the publisher at:**

Executive Excellence Publishing
1344 East 1120 South
Provo, UT 84606
phone: 1-801-375-4060
toll free: 1-800-304-9782
fax: 1-801-377-5960
www.eep.com

For Executive Excellence books, magazines and other products, contact Executive Excellence directly. Call 1-800-304-9782, fax 1-801-377-5960, or visit our Web site at www.eep.com.

Printed in the United States

10 9 8 7 6 5 4 3 2 1

Cover design by Nichole Klein

Printed by Publishers Press

**Library of Congress Cataloging-in-Publication Data**

Bendor-Samuel, Peter, 1960-
  Turning lead into gold : the demystification of outsourcing / by Peter Bendor-Samuel.
    p. cm.
  ISBN 1-890009-87-3 (alk. paper)
  1. Contracting out.  I. Title
  HD2365 .B46 2000
  658.7'2--dc21

                                                00-008590

Every morning in Africa, a gazelle wakes up.
It knows it must run faster than the fastest lion
  or it will be killed.
Every morning in Africa, a lion wakes up.
It knows it must outrun the slowest gazelle
  or it will starve to death.
It doesn't matter whether you are a lion or a gazelle.
When the sun comes up, you'd better be running.

—*The Essence of Survival*

# TABLE OF CONTENTS

   Why Outsourcing Will Change Your Business

   Extracting Wealth from Scrap
   What Exactly Is Outsourcing?
   Misconception of Losing Control
   Outsourcing Is Not Contracting
   The Nature of the Relationship
   Why Outsource?
   What Processes Are Outsourced?
   Cutting to the Core
   Outsourcing as a Solution

Automating the Metrics
Continual Improvement

# Foreword

*by John Staedke*
*President and CEO of BancTec, Inc.*

I've been in the outsourcing industry since 1968. It hasn't always been called "outsourcing," but one company providing its expert services to another company is a well-known, valuable business strategy—no matter what it is called. Outsourcing has some new models today, as is evident by the growing support and need for Application Service Providers. The ASPs and the proliferation of outsourcing to accommodate e-Business strategies serve to reinforce the concept presented in this book: TINA, meaning "There Is No Alternative." Clearly, outsourcing is poised to become even more pervasive in future business models.

Although we have used outsourcing for many years, several questions still surround it. What does it really represent? What is the best way to go about doing it? Can real value be achieved through outsourcing? In this book, Peter Bendor-Samuel addresses these and other questions, adding insight into the subtle, but fundamental, principles of outsourcing. He shows us exactly what we need to know to determine how to outsource, with whom to form an alliance, and how to structure the relationship so both parties achieve the results they set out to achieve.

Not unlike others, I have encountered situations several times in my outsourcing experiences that—to put it mildly—were not appreciated by the customer or supplier. Peter puts his finger right on those problems and explains why they occur. He clearly explains the important principle that customers must define up-front the outcomes they want and then relinquish control of the outsourced processes to the supplier. In my experience, this concept is rarely clear to the customer; and rancor occurs in the relationship because of the frustration that results from this lack of knowledge about how outsourcing works.

Much of current rhetoric represents the parties to an outsourcing agreement as needing to be "partners." Peter reveals that this is not the case, explaining that they have their own separate business objectives, within which they have a common agenda specified by their outsourcing agreement. He points out that struggles occur when one party thinks they are supposed to act as partners when, in reality, they are outsourcing allies.

Peter explains the two concepts about why companies outsource, drawing them together as one point, which is the need to gain or sustain competitive advantage. While economics and the bottom line are often the rationale, he discusses the fact that customers also want improved quality and efficiency in their processes.

While it is often assumed that companies know what their core competencies are, the Internet and new ways to compete are causing those assumptions to be re-examined for validity. Most books about outsourcing don't bring out the fundamental starting point of determining what is core and non-core. Peter highlights the need to narrow the current broad range of processes down to the ones that focus on how the company competes. Today's business models demand speed and flexibility to change. Companies no longer have the financial, human, or even time resources to be expert in all processes.

A good pre-nuptial agreement or a corporate buy-sell agreement needs to be constructed at the outset, while the parties still love each other. The readers of this book will come to understand how to construct an effective contract, establish objective metrics, determine the appropriate length of the contract, ensure the pricing methodology allows the results to be what the customer really hopes to achieve, and how to deal with all the variables in managing outsourcing.

Peter Bendor-Samuel's book about outsourcing differs from others. His overall approach is practical and fundamental, yet this is often not the approach that has been taken historically with outsourcing. Hence, its occasional failures. Often, it has been a love/hate relationship in that the parties really want to do it, but they lack the knowledge needed to handle their incompatibilities. Peter's advice eliminates the possibilities of failure. Rather than recommending an adversarial approach—that is, what is best from the customers' perspective or best from the suppliers' perspective—he presents solutions that allow for a win-win model for both parties. His concepts and strategies lead to a more positive, constructive relationship that furthers the prospects for success for both parties.

Peter Bendor-Samuel is a world-renowned authority who understands exactly what it takes to make outsourcing successful. I met him in the late 1980s, and we have worked together off and on during the years since. I respect his insight and his values-based approach to business. We both enjoy verbal jousting, and neither of us lacks opinions. Over the past 10 years, we have vigorously explored outsourcing and related subjects to determine where we might agree or disagree. During that time, Peter's understanding of the principles of outsourcing has matured well beyond mine. In this book, Peter shares those insights for all who are interested in learning how to make outsourcing successful and how to avoid its pitfalls.

I wish I had discovered these principles earlier and had applied them to my own outsourcing experiences. It would have made life much easier. There is no doubt that this book is a valuable resource, for it presents the fundamental strategies for success in outsourcing. The insights Peter shares in *Turning Lead Into Gold* definitely will enable you to mine the value in your outsourcing relationships.

# Introduction

*"A man who carries a cat by the tail learns something he can learn in no other way."*
—Mark Twain

A powerful tool has swept across the North American business landscape and now is expanding globally. That dynamic tool is outsourcing. During the past decade of its explosive, worldwide growth, corporate managers and executives have come to understand the applicability of outsourcing to their companies. A host of businesses have recognized and acknowledged its significance; they have discovered that outsourcing creates value.

Outsourcing holds great potential for those who learn how to apply its principles effectively. Conversely, there are deep pitfalls for those who attempt to use this powerful tool without first learning those principles. As someone who has for many years "carried the cat by the tail" (as a supplier, a buyer and now as a consultant), I have written this book to share what I have learned so that you won't have to experience those same mistakes and misfortunes. This book will help you understand how outsourcing works—what it is, how and when to use it, how to apply effective outsourcing principles to your business, and how to profit from it. In short, this book demystifies outsourcing.

The book illustrates the strategic thinking that makes outsourcing profitable. With this "map," business managers and executives can avoid taking wrong turns and making poor decisions based on mistaken theories. Employees who are being swept up in the maelstrom of business reorganization will also understand what is happening to them and why it is a good thing.

The book also gives direction to the practitioner. It holds advice for executives who seek to transform their organizations by becoming outsourcing suppliers. It enables those already in outsourcing relationships to gain greater value from them. Finally, it explains to investors why and how companies are creating value through outsourcing.

This book is more than a manual on how to structure outsourcing relationships. It is a survival guide. In it, I present the theories and principles behind outsourcing, describing in detail which ones work and which ones don't—and why. Understanding these principles is a key to making outsourcing work.

This book is divided into two sections. Part 1 is about TINA, an acronym for "There Is No Alternative." Indeed, for companies that plan to survive and thrive in the new global, connected economy, there is no alternative to outsourcing. Chapter 1 is a blueprint for survival in a world where business decisions can be activated at lightning speed with the click of a mouse. Chapter 2 explains what outsourcing is and why you need to use this tool. In

Chapter 3, I discuss the historical development of outsourcing; and in Chapter 4, I address how leverage creates value.

Part 2, "Principles in Action," is a business guide for those who are ready to cross the chasm and enter this brave new world. In life, knowledge is often gained from learning about other people's mistakes. I begin Chapter 5 with a discussion of some common traps that buyers and suppliers have fallen into, then we move to how to build flexibility into the relationship and how to make additional contributions. Chapter 6 explains the process of establishing service levels and metrics; Chapter 7 continues this discussion with a focus on pricing, including how to establish and adjust prices. Perquisites for success, as well as common practices that inhibit the creation of value, are explained in Chapter 8. In Chapter 9, I examine the various structural approaches to an alliance and how to build a sustainable contract. Finally, I sum up the promise of outsourcing in Chapter 10.

Like it or not, outsourcing is here to stay. It is already the foundation of the global, connected economy. It was once a strategic tool. Today, the Internet has made outsourcing the pervasive paradigm. You may choose to ignore it, but you do so at your own peril—because your competitors are not ignoring it. My hope is that you will apply the principles I share in this book and use outsourcing—much like the medieval alchemists—to turn lead into gold.

*Part*
# ONE

---

# THERE IS
# NO ALTERNATIVE

# Chapter 1

# Embracing TINA

*"I think there is a world market for maybe five computers."*
— Thomas Watson, chairman of IBM, 1943

In 1943 when Thomas Watson spoke those fateful words about the potential global market for computers, he did not appreciate that the world was on the brink of a technology-driven revolution in which he and his company were to play a starring role. Now in a new millennium, we face a transformation driven by the Internet, a technology that is certain to change the way the world does business. Information, money, and even services move across the planet with the click of a mouse. Business cycles that used to require months now have been reduced to minutes in today's e-driven marketplace.

As we think about the implications of this new technology-driven revolution, it is clear that every organization faces an uncertain future with the pace of change placing an ever-increasing strain on senior managers. Faced with new dimensions of competition, organizations find that there is only time to focus on what they do best. Most companies can't afford the time or financial resources to concentrate on every function or process necessary to run their business. Yet, in this time of ever-increasing competition, low-cost operations and operational excellence in all facets of the company are essential now more than ever.

To solve this apparent paradox, many organizations have turned to the 30-year-old tool of outsourcing as the best way to survive and even thrive in the nascent world of e-business. By divesting themselves of their non-core processes, organizations are able to improve the level of service, cut costs and free up time and capital to concentrate on what is most important—how they differentiate themselves and compete. As more organizations work through the implications of this new world order, they find no alternative—except to join the ever-growing ranks that utilize outsourcing.

## The Formula for Turning Lead into Gold

The most successful survival tactic will be to concentrate on how to create value and eliminate the other distractions. This is not to say that all the processes we need to ignore are not essential or that we can do without them. A non-core process is a necessary component of an organization. We cannot do without such processes as human resources, accounting or information technology. If we are to stay in business and prosper, they must be done extremely well; however, because a process is important does not make it core. Core competencies are "the soul of the company," according to C.K. Prahalad, a professor at the University of Michigan Business School, who coined the term in 1990. They include the skills and technology unique to an organization. They create the strengths that pay the bills and position a company to attack new markets.

Outsourcing has become an accepted business tool because companies of all sizes and shapes have recognized that they can become more profitable and stay on the cutting edge of change by turning over those other tasks to companies that consider them their core competencies.

## TINA: There Is No Alternative

I was first introduced to TINA on a cruise ship during a business seminar given by a scenario planner from the Global Business Network. At dinner after his remarkable presentation, we discussed future scenarios most likely facing the world. He described to me a series of forces, which he believes now give the world's major economies no choice but to open up their markets to competition. He called the combination of these forces TINA, an acronym, meaning, "There Is No Alternative." I was immediately enamored of this concept and its implications to my profession of outsourcing, and I have unabashedly appropriated it.

Organizations around the world face increasingly competitive markets. If they are to flourish, I believe they must adopt outsourcing in some measure. There is no alternative. No organization, however well managed or well financed, will be able to cope as competitive demands for its cycle time (or the time it takes to respond to customers' requests) moves from two months to two hours. The need to improve every aspect of an organization while increasing focus on its core processes will make outsourcing as foundational to competing successfully in the Internet Age as is access to the Internet itself.

Outsourcing is the only tool available that provides the ability to improve operations while cutting costs and releasing capital and time that can then be used on those core areas. For an increasing number of organizations, there is no alternative to adopting outsourcing's principles.

# Chapter 2

# THE ALCHEMIST'S DREAM

*"The value of anything is not what you paid for it, nor what it cost to produce, but what you can get for it at an auction."*
—William Lyon Phelps, educator

Learned scholars during the Middle Ages devoted hundreds of years in zealous pursuit of the legendary "philosopher's stone." Not a rock, it was a substance reputed to have had the capability of turning base metals into gold, the most perfect metal. It was believed in those days that a preparation of gold would cure all ills. Scholars dedicated their lives to the study of alchemy, conducting countless experiments in hopes of discovering the right formula for transforming seemingly worthless substances into gold.

Their followers also sought the secret formula,

but their intent was to create vast wealth for themselves from gold. Today, people still pursue a means of generating wealth and value from sources of seemingly little worth. Some have achieved amazing success on a scale far greater than the medieval alchemists ever could have dreamed.

On a visit to Cripple Creek in Colorado (the site of the fourth largest gold-producing mine in the world at the turn of the 20th century), I visited an organization working in the mountains of old slag, which had been discarded during earlier decades of gold mining. The company had developed a new process to extract gold from the waste product left behind by the earlier miners. It was an impressive display of modern alchemy, yet it pales in significance when compared to the wealth being generated by today's vast and growing outsourcing movement.

The modern alchemy of outsourcing generates immense wealth from business functions that traditionally have been regarded as expenses or drags on earnings—slag piling up. Outsourcing transforms expenses into profit centers and, just as in medieval times, turns lead into gold. Observers have taken note of the new value created and want to know more about this phenomenon. Although outsourcing is not founded in a secret formula, it is built upon specific principles and revolves around important strategies that definitely affect the value and the success of the results. Without these vital components, outsourcing easily can be misunderstood and, consequently, will fail.

**What Exactly Is Outsourcing?**

Outsourcing takes place when an organization transfers the ownership of a business process to a supplier. The key to this definition is the concept of *transfer of control.* This definition differentiates outsourcing from business relationships in which the buyer retains control of the process or, in other words, tells the supplier how to do the work. It is the transfer of ownership that defines outsourcing and often makes it such a challenging, painful process. In outsourcing, the buyer does not instruct the supplier how to perform its task but, instead, focuses on communicating what results it wants to buy; it leaves the process of accomplishing those results to the supplier.

In many outsourcing agreements, the supplier provides the buyer with services or processes that the buyer previously performed internally. When a buyer hands over a process to a supplier, it also hands over the responsibility to determine if the tasks involved are appropriate, and, if appropriate, how they should be executed. The appropriateness and how-to decisions belong to the supplier.

For an outsourcing buyer, the key is to focus on the results of the process. The nature of the beast is that the supplier controls the process.

Consider a hypothetical instance where an automobile manufacturer decides to outsource the production of engines. The manufacturer had been painting the engines with an expensive paint purchased from a local manufacturer because the process and supplies contributed to its community. But the outsourcing supplier might decide to discontinue using that kind of paint.

A supplier might not necessarily have the same compunctions for continuing certain features of a business process that a buyer may have found necessary. For instance, a supplier might discontinue generating reports for all non-economic processes that were produced and sent to the head office. While the buyer was required to do so because its lender wanted to track the money used by the buyer under its loan covenants, the supplier would have no connection to the buyer's lender and no need to produce the reports.

What happened at Simpson Industries in its outsourcing relationship with IBM Global Services is a good example of the all-important concept of process ownership. Simpson is a global supplier to the automotive industry and to diesel engine customers. It is not in business to operate computers. That's why Simpson turned to IBM for the computer expertise it needed.

Simpson's executive team was specific about the metrics it required. A crucial requirement was that the computers stay up and the applications stay running seven days a week, 24 hours a day to eliminate wasted downtime. This was something Simpson could never do in-house.

Reducing scheduled computer maintenance was another goal. Prior to the outsourcing engagement, the computer was down every night for four hours (eight hours on the weekend) for backup activity. As soon as IBM took over the process, it recommended a different backup strategy. The new way of doing things slashed computer downtime to about five hours per week.

Dick LeFebvre, director of information technology for Simpson Industries, says that the relationship has exceeded his expectations. LeFebvre acknowledges that the floor space in the manufacturing facility occupied by the computer work could have been better utilized for manufacturing, so the decision to outsource was an easy one. "If there is somebody out there who can do it better, faster, and cheaper than you, then you don't want to do the work in-house. If it doesn't make sense, you outsource it," he says.

For Simpson, the outsourcing relationship definitely has made sense. The computer is located at IBM Global Services' facility in Rochester, New York, and supports nine Simpson locations. IBM personnel operate this system alongside systems for other companies. The supplier created internal alarms and indicators so that, if Simpson's system were to go down, it would get immediate attention. This is a part of the "true value" of the deal for Simpson. The supplier provides the buyer with a worry-free IT environment by using a process that runs itself and requires little extraordinary intervention.

## Misconception of Losing Control

LeFebvre says it is absurd for a Chief Information Officer to think, "If I outsource this, I'll lose control." Control is not lost in an outsourcing relationship; only the means of control has changed. In outsourcing, the control of the process belongs to the supplier. The buyer exchanges its ability to dictate how the process will be performed for the ability to define the results and hold the supplier accountable for them. If the outsourcing agreement is structured properly, using the principles detailed in this book, the supplier's control will generate value for both parties.

The concept of process ownership is the single most misunderstood concept in outsourcing. It is a mistake for a buyer to outsource a process and still attempt to dictate the process. This exchange of control within the process is a source of value because, invariably, the supplier possesses more process expertise than the buyer. A buyer that tries to dictate how a process should work would be giving advice to one who is more expert in a particular area than the buyer is. In doing so, the buyer would be undoing the supplier's accountability for the results of the process—perhaps one of the most valuable elements of outsourcing. It is a mistake for a buyer to outsource a process and still attempt to dictate the process. Returning to our alchemy analogy, it is the transfer of ownership that is the necessary chemical agent that allows lead (non-core processes) to be converted into gold.

The government of South Australia, one of the seven states in Australia, realized it needed someone else with expertise to handle non-core processes. Severe mismanagement under a previous administration saw the state's bank lose in excess of AUD $4.5 billion through bad loans around the world. Since the state owned the bank, the state had to make good on the debts. This caused economic problems, which led to a change of government in late 1993.

The new ministers decided one of the best ways to reinvigorate the economy was to outsource the government's information technology (IT) functions. The Aussies chose EDS as the state's "preferred strategic partner" for a nine-year contract. In essence, the ministers outsourced the entire government! EDS' first task was to amalgamate the work of 140 separate agencies. It had to provide services to 83 government departments in over 1,000 locations. It was easier for a professional, an outsider, to come in and rearrange for maximum efficiency. Today there are just 10 "super"agencies that take care of the government's business. In addition to saving the government of South Australia more than $100 million in computing costs over the life of the contract, the outsourcing initiatives have spurred economic development in the local IT industry and have produced cost savings for local businesses needing IT solutions. The change in control frees the supplier to create the value that both sides seek in outsourcing.

Although micro-management is not advisable, a totally free hand is not the solution, either. Lack of the right kind of management is equally bad. Cy Sairam, head of applications development for Paragon Solutions, an Indian IT outsourcer in Bangalore, suggests that buyers tap a member of senior management and add a new position called "relationship manager." This executive would monitor and manage the outsourcing relationship and have the power to resolve any issues that might arise.

**Outsourcing Is Not Contracting**

The subtle distinctions underlying the definitions of "outsourcing" and "contracting" are the reason for much of the complexity that plagues outsourcing. The challenges and value that outsourcing can deliver also lie within this subtle definition.

One way to explain outsourcing is to define what it is not. Contracting is the purchasing of goods or services when the buyer owns the process. If the buyer owns a process but purchases time, products or services to facilitate that process, then the buyer is in a contractual relationship. If the supplier owns the process, then the buyer is probably outsourcing.

The elements in relationships are treated differently according to whether the relationship is outsourcing or contracting, as follows.

*Initial Process Ownership Investments.* When an outsourcing supplier develops or operates a process, it makes investments in equipment and infrastructure. This requires significantly greater costs than are necessary in contracting. All things being equal, in a comparison of a series of contracts for items that together make up a process (as opposed to items that cover the entire process in outsourcing), the costs for the latter will be higher. This is so if for no other reason than the fact that the buyer will have to replace the process expertise if it decides to return the process to an in-house operation.

One good example of the investments an outsourcing supplier makes on behalf of a buyer's process is the e-commerce Web site that Plaut Consulting created for Cavalier Homes, one of the nation's largest manufacturers and distributors of manufactured housing. The Alabama manufacturer wanted to expand its market, so it turned to Plaut to design a new marketing channel. Plaut designed and created a portal to meet Cavalier's business objectives. The first objective was to assist Cavalier's many satisfied customers who needed repair or replacement parts for their homes. Electrical and plumbing parts for such housing are very unique and are not readily available. Now Cavalier's homeowners can order the parts they need from the Web site.

The second objective was Cavalier's dealers. The Web site provides a more efficient way for dealers to place their orders. Making all the variations that go into a manufactured home be available on the Web site has sped up a time-consuming process. Finally, Cavalier has other businesses, which include homeowner's insurance, home financing and satellite dish sales for Direct TV. Any visitor can purchase these services from the Cavalier portal.

Plaut maintains the portal for Cavalier. It was already handling the company's back office financial functions on an outsourcing basis when Cavalier determined it was time to enter the e-commerce fray. Plaut added e-commerce to this technology backbone.

If Cavalier were to become dissatisfied with its outsourcing relationship with Plaut and decide to return the process in-house, it would have to start from scratch to build the portal infrastructure and processes that its supplier now owns.

*Switching Costs.* Having control over a contracting relationship is a fairly accepted part of Western business culture. In most contracting situations, the buyer is able to replace its suppliers without too much cost or resistance. In outsourcing, where the buyer gives up control of the process, the buyer usually will face significantly increased costs if it decides to switch suppliers. In a contracting situation, most companies believe they can use their position as a consumer and switch suppliers fairly quickly and easily. But to go into outsourcing with that assumption is a big mistake!

In the event of an early termination of the relationship, the supplier's switching costs (often embedded in the transaction) usually become the responsibility of the buyer. In addition to termination charges, if the buyer decides to resume responsibility for the process itself, it would be necessary to rebuild its infrastructure and recapture the process expertise. This can be costly and may not be easy to do. The buyer also would have to replace the capital investment, time and materials, because the supplier would have begun to integrate these into its own supply chain.

We saw an example at the Everest Group, our consulting division. Anthem, a Blue Cross-Blue Shield healthcare insurer in Indianapolis, Indiana, was unhappy with its mainframe computer outsourcer and was considering bringing the process back in-house. The cost, which was in excess of $60 million, included the computer hardware and software as well as the construction costs for the data center itself. But that cost was trivial compared to the risk involved in establishing a world-class IT processing group from scratch. At this stage, they had none of that expertise already on board and would have to recruit all of the IT group.

Anthem decided the task was too daunting. Quality information is the soul of Anthem's business. The insurance company did not want to trust this mission critical function to an untried staff in a new data center. The risk was just too great. The company began looking for a new IT outsourcer that already had the facilities, equipment and staff.

***Measuring Results.*** Different things are measured in outsourcing than are measured in contracting. When a buyer controls the process, the buyer measures the compliance with its instructions and completion of tasks or components. In other words, the buyer measures the end result. Citing an example from the automobile industry, we are concerned that we buy a quality automobile, rather than a quality drive shaft.

*Length of Relationship.* The initial process investment costs, together with the possibility of high switching costs, leads to longer-term relationships in outsourcing than in contracting. Because of these costs in an outsourcing relationship, the economic power shifts to the supplier. The longer the contract is continued, the more this power shift continues. A would-be buyer or supplier needs to keep this principle in mind; it will be fully discussed later in Chapter 5.

*Supplier Power.* Because suppliers own the outsourced process and buyers face substantial switching costs, suppliers often enjoy greater market power than they would as contractors.

## The Nature of the Relationship

Participants in an outsourcing relationship are not partners; they are allies. The term "partners" implies joint ownership, a permanent relationship (bound like a marriage), whether good or bad. Allies, on the other hand, act together for the benefit of each other in many spheres and instances where their common interests match. Their relationship is longstanding but not permanent; in fact, where their interests do not match, they are not allied. Outsourcing alliances are much like the countries in NATO, for example. They cooperate as allies from time to time (in Desert Storm and Kosovo, for instance); yet they have been enemies at one time or another in the past and continue their skirmishes today, typically on the trade front. The British and the French have argued about beef, and Europeans don't want to eat American genetically engineered corn. These alliances are fluid and are based on each country's interests.

Some outsourcing relationships never progress beyond the exchange of money for the services. Others, however, expand into ever-increasing areas for value creation. Not every relationship can be made into such an alliance; but where the participants take on the characteristics of allies, they have a potentially enormous amount of value they otherwise would not have been able to obtain. Outsourcing is built on a foundation of such an alliance.

### Why Outsource?

Following are the reasons why businesses most often choose to outsource some of their processes. At times, these reasons work in combination with one another. Companies outsource:

- to reduce and control operating costs
- to improve company focus
- to improve quality
- to access capabilities not otherwise available
- to free internal resources for other purposes

- to reduce cycle time
- to make capital funds available
- to obtain cash infusion
- to reduce risk
- to gain flexibility
- to turn fixed costs into variable costs
- to stabilize an unstable situation
- to engage an outside agent of change.

The most frequent reason for outsourcing is to reduce operating costs. In my involvement with hundreds of outsourcing transactions, I can count on one hand the times when cost was not important in the decision to outsource. For those who say that outsourcing is moving away from cost as its principal driver, I suggest they look at the source of the pressure to outsource. Determine who is making the statement and, in most cases, I predict that it will be an enthusiastic supplier wanting to increase margins.

If a buyer cannot receive an improved economic position as a result of its outsourcing decision, then it should not outsource. Cost reduction is central to almost all outsourcing transactions—and certainly all of the successful ones. This does not necessarily mean that buyers will spend less money than they did before the outsourcing began. It is quite possible that they will receive a superior or more timely service by outsourcing and would spend more money for that service; but it ought to be less money than it would cost the buyer to do it in-house. When it costs the buyer more, deep dissatisfaction predictably will develop on the part of the buyer.

The other frequent reason to outsource is the buyer's desire to concentrate the focus of the organization on more important areas. Companies find that if they can identify and focus on their core processes and functions, and allow other companies (which are expert in a process) to perform the non-core processes or aspects of the business, they begin to thrive. By outsourcing non-core functions, the buyer can tap into more competence, energy and ideas. The supplier can do the job better—not because it is smarter—but because it has more minds thinking about that particular element of the business (logistics or IT, for example). The supplier can be tapped for creativity, new ideas and investments. Maybe the buyer can even leverage the investments elsewhere later on.

### What Processes Are Outsourced?

In outsourcing, a buyer outsources one or more processes that are not core to its business but are essential to its operation. For example, Nike has long outsourced the manufacturing of its popular footwear. The company understands that its core business is not the manufacturing of sneakers but, rather, the design and marketing of sneakers. It uses outsourcing suppliers for the entire manufacturing process.

Much of high-tech computer manufacturing these days is outsourced, and the same people who make power supplies for Sun Microsystems one day might be making them for Hewlett-Packard the next day. A construction company might decide to outsource its desktop functions since its employees know more about building codes than computer codes. A healthcare organization might outsource its facilities maintenance since its employees need to take the patients' temperatures and not manage the interior thermostat.

Although it occurs infrequently, buyers have been known to find that an outsourced function was really core and then need to re-assimilate it. But, by definition, if a process is outsourced, we may assume that the management team decided that the process was non-core. The buyer may outsource important, even strategic, functions; but it comes as a result of the buyer's management team having decided that it will focus on functions that are more core to the company's essential reason to exist. Or, it may decide to take advantage of the cost savings, improved time to market, or other advantages that a supplier can offer for outsourced functions. "Non-core" does not mean "not important." It just means "not the single most important."

Comdata is an excellent example of how a company recognized its need to outsource a non-core function and how its supplier allowed Comdata to grow and flourish in ways it could not otherwise have achieved. In fact, the Outsourcing Center was so impressed with Comdata's relationship with IBM we awarded them an *Outsourcing Journal* Editor's

Choice Award in 1999.

When a long-haul truck pulls in for a fuel fill up, the driver charges the $150 gas bill on a credit card. More than 15,000 fleet operators rely on Comdata to provide these credit cards for their truck drivers. Outsourcing the credit card charges eliminated record keeping, tracking and reconciling thousands of credit card receipts. Comdata verifies and pays the bills, then forwards an invoice with a small mark-up to its clients. Therefore, Comdata's data network must be reliable, accurate, secure and always available. Because Comdata's fee is small, relative to the amount of each purchase, cash flow is extremely important to its well being.

Comdata decided to outsource its IT function to IBM Global Services. The outsourced functions include hardware, operations, applications development, network design and operation, management and maintenance. IBM has a facility that is entirely dedicated to Comdata.

Although the network and data processing functions are vital to Comdata's business, they are not core operations. By outsourcing, the buyer's management and investments can now be focused on core matters, even though IBM controls this important function.

I once had a spirited discussion with Shane McEwen, a strategy consultant in Australia. The topic of our conversation was how to define what is a core process and how to differentiate those from non-core, yet important, processes. After some time, during which we both struggled to produce a concise definition, Shane said, "I can identify and differentiate both kinds of processes for any company—but only after I have gone through a very complex, lengthy and expensive consulting project." Obviously, he intended this as a joke. The truth is that Shane is an honest man of great integrity who would not exploit his customers.

The deeper truth lies in the fact that the nature of what is "core" is dependent on several factors, which vary for each organization and which change over time. As Shane pointed out, "Core processes are tied to the way in which a company generates shareholder value. They are a factor of an organization's competitive situation and are the true tools it uses to differentiate itself from its competitors." As such, core processes will change over time—when competition and new technologies bring change to the value chain and companies evolve to maximize their value among new conditions.

The reason why this distinction of what is core is so important is that those processes are the soul of a company and cannot be for sale at any price. Not understanding this fact will court disaster for a company. Because of today's competitive environment with its constant need to reinvent process, no company can master all of its important processes all of the time. This forces companies to choose which processes should have executive focus and resources devoted to them. McEwen closed our debate with the key reason to learn the distinction of what is core. A company that has defined its core processes can use this knowledge to further its profitability and maximize its return to its investors. The ongoing process of defining what is core to a company is the engine behind a good deal of today's outsourcing market.

**Cutting to the Core**

There are several good examples of companies defining what is "core." The ability to manufacture is core to DaimlerChrysler, but the manufacturing of seat covers is not; so it outsources the manufacture of seat covers. The company's identity is not tied up in manufacturing; it is defined by its ability to master design, integration of sub-components and management of the distribution in marketing cars. At one time, the disciplines of manufacturing component parts may have been a core process, but the company has moved beyond this and now competes on new factors.

For the large U.S. retail chain, Saks Fifth Avenue, whether its customers have private label Saks cards is an important strategic component to the store's business. The card attracts customers and allows the company to tie its customers more closely to it through customer loyalty programs. The process by which the cards are issued and serviced, however, is not core to Saks' business.

The ability to build innovative products of high quality is core to Cisco Systems. However, the process of manufacturing these products is not core.

Cisco is a poster child for the new reality of focusing on core competencies only. Although it dominates the market for routers and other Internet-enabling technology, it does not own a single manufacturing plant. Instead, it outsources all of its manufacturing needs so it can focus on designing and marketing new products.

Often, a company outsources a process that might otherwise be considered core; but it does so because it lacks economy of scale in that process. (An economy of scale happens when the marginal cost is less than the unit cost. If you already have a process in place, it costs less to produce another unit.) In doing so, the company has realized it competes on some other element. For example, British Airways now competes on its marketing ability, its routes and its access to capital. It now outsources all other functions (ticketing, check-in and baggage handling, for example), and the airline even leases its planes. British Airways has redefined its core.

Another excellent example of a company redefining its core business is British Petroleum (BP). This company realized that traditional functions, which many companies have historically viewed as core (such as accounting and human resources), are not what it competes on. BP's core competency is its ability to find oil and to establish retail networks for petrochemical products.

At BP, outsourcing has come to be a central tactic in the strategy of running a lean, flat organization. In an industry populated by many of the world's largest enterprises, it is not easy to stay nimble. Success in the exploration and production of oil and gas requires quick response to changes, whether in the form of unpredictable price fluctuations, extreme variations in supply, or in dramatic shifts in demand (such as those that took place in the Asian economic crisis in the 1990s). BP has relied on outsourcing to gain efficiency in its operations, minimize costs, and keep to a strategy of staying lean, flexible and responsive.

The practical implication is that non-core business functions are at a disadvantage when competing for senior management attention and support. Another consideration is the fact that career opportunities for accounting and related legal experts within an oil and gas production operation are more limited than within an organization devoted to those functions. BP concluded that outsourcing those functions would provide career development opportunities, as well as benefit its strategy for gaining efficiency, reducing cost, and maintaining a high level of expertise.

BP selected an experienced supplier with knowledge and presence in the region—Pricewaterhouse-Coopers (PwC). It had substantial experience in business process outsourcing (BPO) with BP's European operations. PwC understood the buyer's culture, operating requirements, procedures and reporting requirements; and it was eager to expand operations in Columbia and Venezuela. BP acknowledges that it was confident of PwC's thorough understanding of the most efficient and appropriate processes and systems for the buyer. It was also confident that PwC could anticipate and manage any changes that would be required.

The results have been pleasing for both organizations. A joint review board meets quarterly to examine performance against objectives, as detailed in the service level agreement. The board also identifies areas of opportunity for improvement, resolves issues, and revises service level performance criteria, if necessary. The meetings ensure that learning is shared between both parties.

Several factors have been instrumental in this successful working relationship. In particular, the involvement of the senior partners of PwC in London provided drive and vigor to the new arrangement. As in most business situations, much depends on building a good relationship with each other. The strength of the relationship at the senior levels helped both parties to stay focused on the strategic objectives. This is especially important during the heat of battle when issues arise. Steps must be taken early in the relationship to keep the team committed to making an outsourcing deal work.

BP intends to continue to build on its successful strategy of outsourcing non-core functions where practical because of the value already experienced to date from its ability to focus on its core business functions.

## Outsourcing as a Solution

Outsourcing has gone beyond alchemy. Unlike the alchemists, who sought to utilize forces they did not understand, with outsourcing we are able to identify how to turn lead into gold and fully understand the principles underpinning this surprising transformation.

There is no magic list of processes or functions that a company should outsource. The important elements are that it should be a non-core process and that the company should gain a real and sustainable advantage. Some would argue that a company should outsource all non-core functions and processes; indeed, this may become the standard in the future. At this point in time, though, most organizations are still experimenting with outsourcing and outsource only small parts of their overall infrastructure. Often, these are data processing or areas enabled by data processing but, increasingly, other kinds of processes are being outsourced. The following examples illustrate the types of processes that are often outsourced today, as well as some of the motivations behind the decisions to do so.

A world-class capability in telecommunications management is a classic example of a reason to outsource. Companies, both in the U.S. and abroad, have found it difficult in recent years to retain high-level telecommunications talent; it has become a very scarce commodity. Telecommunications managers tend not to desire to work for large industrial companies and prefer, instead, to work in the more glamorous high-tech industries. AT&T Solutions, for example, is a supplier that meets these needs. Its employees perceive it as being a dynamic, fast-growing, high-tech company that attracts and retains world-class telecommunications managers. Many buyers have entered into outsourcing agreements with AT&T Solutions because they no longer feel capable of performing the telecommunications work in-house.

J.P. Morgan & Co. Incorporated is a wonderful example of a company that used outsourcing so it could better utilize its own staff. In the late 1990s, it retained the Pinnacle Alliance (composed of Computer Sciences Corporation [CSC], Andersen Consulting, AT&T Solutions and Bell Atlantic Corporation) to take over what it viewed as non-core data processing functions. The company's major reason for outsourcing was to be able to redirect some of its talented staff into its investment banking practice, which was its core activity.

A number of successful outsourcing relationships have been based around the reengineering of business processes. These often have information technology components (such as implementation of data processing systems, applications and products—SAP projects). Buyers approach outsourcing suppliers (such as PwC or Ernst & Young LLP) that specialize in the reengineering of business organizations and choose suppliers that have undisputed process expertise in the area to be reengineered. The primary value proposition here is for the supplier to reengineer the process so as to deliver superior results.

Outsourcing also creates value for a buyer when it is used as a solution for seemingly intractable business problems (although few companies wish to admit this). Companies have decided to outsource functions that have been out of control and have resisted management's sustained efforts to fix them. Western Union Financial Services, Inc. used outsourcing in this manner when, in the mid-1980s, the company experienced high employee turnover as it went into Chapter 11 bankruptcy. By outsourcing some processes (and the staff performing them) to Electronic Data Systems (EDS), Western Union allowed its employees to work for a more attractive company. In so doing, the end result was a stabilization of the high turnover rate of personnel, which had threatened to end all hope of a successful turnaround from bankruptcy.

Outsourcing is also an excellent means of solving a company's lack of flexibility due to large fixed costs. These costs exist, whether business is up or down. Outsourcing can allow a company to match its costs to its revenue, which is especially advantageous for businesses that are seasonal, cyclical or experiencing high growth. When combined with the redeployment of capital, this ability to turn fixed costs into variable ones allows a company to match what it spends on services to its revenue streams. This avoids the significant overhead of fixed costs.

Hallmark Cards Inc., the greeting card company, faced this problem. Over three million card buyers phone its 800 number every year, but fourth-quarter phone calls account for almost 50 percent of that annual volume. Hiring holiday workers was a big headache for Hallmark.

Hallmark outsourced its call center to Convergys Corporation, which now fields 100 percent of Hallmark's calls. Although callers believe they are talking to Hallmark staffers, Convergys employees handle consumer queries, address complaints and record comments.

Convergys now has the responsibility of forecasting staffing needs for Hallmark's call center, making sure the center has enough operators to answer the phones during the busy fourth quarter but not too many on the roster during the slower first quarter. Hallmark executives estimate this outsourcing relationship saves the company $1 million a year in payroll expenses.

Outsourcing gives buyers a cost-effective way to acquire cutting edge technology. Rob Krolik is the chief financial officer for karna LLC, a California company that sells a high-resolution mouse needed for computer games. He wanted to run his accounting functions using Oracle's Financial System. He estimates it would have cost karna over $1 million to purchase the Oracle program. By outsourcing the financial process to ReSourcePhoenix, a financial Application Service Provider (ASP), karna pays just $200,000 a year to its outsourcing supplier to run its books on Oracle.

## Modern Alchemy

Companies facing increased competition for foreign markets must now look to their core competencies and differentiate between what is a core process and what is important but not core. They must then seek to improve their business processes and look for faster, less expensive ways to perform those processes. For many companies, outsourcing is the solution. It holds the potential to accomplish what seems impossible—to create value where none exists.

## Chapter 3

# THE TRAIL TO OUTSOURCING

*"The result meant much more to me than the mere*
*successful realization of an experiment.*
*It was an epoch in history."*
—Gelmo Marconi, in his report on receiving the
first radio signal across the Atlantic in 1901

These days, outsourcing is a familiar business practice recognizable to almost everyone. It is feared by unions and middle management, condemned on the pages of newspaper editorial sections, and praised by stock analysts. But it has not always been so well known.

No one knows when the first business process was outsourced. Perhaps it was very early, at the start of the Industrial Revolution when companies started to specialize; or perhaps it was ushered in with Adam Smith's book, *The Wealth of Nations*. Until recently, neither of these instances was recognized as the phenomenon we know today as outsourcing.

The 1960s saw the rise of specialized companies that promoted their identities as being able to take on and run processes for other organizations. The rise in awareness in the ranks of senior management that such a tool as outsourcing exists and is appropriate for more than the most menial tasks has occurred only during the 1990s.

### The First Pioneer

Ross Perot is widely credited with starting the outsourcing movement when he founded his company, Electronic Data Systems. The story of his founding of EDS has become a legend.

A successful salesman for IBM, Perot became dissatisfied with its policy of capping his commission. After one particularly successful first quarter, during which he reached all his targets for the entire year, he quit and decided to try something new. With only $1,000 of his own money, he searched the country for a company that would share his vision and allow him to provide it with services, rather than equipment (which the company would provide for itself). Frito-Lay provided him with that first opportunity.

From there, he built on his success, adding new customers and buying spare processing time from companies that had excess production capacity. It was not long before he developed his own infrastructure and started building economies of scale through owning and operating his own data centers. His early recognition of the necessity for economies of scale allowed his customers to save money while he made significant profits for his own company. In the process, he discovered the gold mine of outsourcing.

EDS went on to add customers in many different industries, and it is significant that most of them had an important similarity. Most were "an ox in a ditch"—that is, a company waiting to be rescued from a dilemma which it despaired of being able to resolve on its own. Each one had failed repeatedly to manage its data processing operations adequately; this had resulted in excessive costs and poor service to their customers. The companies' senior management had found it necessary to look outside their companies for a solution.

As EDS expanded, it found that an increasing number of its customers were in regulated industries such as Medicaid and Medicare. Their operations and procedures were very similar because they all had to comply with the same regulatory requirements. Having noted this degree of standardization among its customers, EDS built broader offerings, encompassing more of its customers' processes, and thus creating still greater economies of scale.

Offerings like these soon become the core moneymakers for EDS. From there, the company targeted other regulated businesses such as banks and credit unions. Then it expanded into non-regulated industries. It was able to do so because of the huge economies of scale it had generated in the areas of data centers, networks and business process engineering.

### Others Followed the EDS Trail

Other companies noticed the economic success of EDS, and soon there were new entrants in the outsourcing field. Large banks, such as Pittsburgh's Mellon Bank Corporation, began to leverage their own processing expertise and formidable scale to establish their own outsourcing supplier companies. Shortly thereafter, companies such as CSC started to specialize as outsourcing suppliers for government agencies.

CSC's outsourcing agreement with General Dynamics (GD) provides a good look back at the business environment in the early days. At the end of the 1980s, defense contractor GD was a $10 billion company. Its Data Systems Division had roughly 2,500 employees supporting the company's data systems. Then the Berlin Wall tumbled, the Cold War ended, and the U.S. government's defense budget shrank. GD faced the need to focus on its profitable core businesses.

"We realized that we were going to be divesting some of the units we had," says Ken Hill, vice president, information technology. "The biggest entanglement that we had during that time was IT, because all of the operating groups were supported by the Data Systems Division."

The company decided to try to sell off the division with the provision that the new owner take over all of the employees and have those people continue to support IT for GD. In November 1991, such a deal was struck. On a Friday, people were General Dynamics employees. Then, on the next Monday, they were sitting at the same desk, but they were CSC employees.

At the same time, GD and CSC signed a 10-year contract for the vendor to provide IT outsourcing support. The deal has since been extended by three years, through the end of 2004. The original deal gave CSC an assured business base over a 10-year period and also provided entry into companies that were acquiring other business units from GD.

Many companies attempted to enter the outsourcing field as suppliers at that time, but few of them remain. What differentiated EDS from most of its early imitators was its insistence on taking over a business process rather than just providing a data center or other services. Those companies that focused only on economy of scale (such as a data center) failed. EDS and a few other true outsourcing suppliers like Automatic Data Processing Inc. (ADP) survived and prospered. In payroll services, ADP found a process for which it could build unparalleled expertise and significant economies of scale. It has become one of the world's most successful and enduring outsourcing suppliers.

## Outsourcing Enters the Mainstream

The big breakthrough for outsourcing came when IBM entered the outsourcing market in the area of data processing. IBM's market leadership and dominance in data processing was increasingly threatened because its large client base engaged in long-term contracts with EDS. Although under these contracts EDS had become the purchaser of equipment and software for these companies, the customers were relentless in efforts to give a significant portion of their business processes to competitors in order to ensure price competition. IBM structured a new subsidiary and boldly entered the outsourcing market.

The entry of IBM gave a strength and legitimacy to outsourcing that it had previously lacked. IBM was, at that time, not only the pre-eminent provider of IT services; it was also one of the world's most trusted companies. IBM had a reputation for integrity and ability to deliver solutions that was unmatched by any other company. Just four years earlier, IBM had transformed the PC industry in much the same manner. Its reputation gave legitimacy to that new technology, and IBM established standards others could build on. Now, by offering outsourcing services, it placed its stamp of approval on this new form of business and thereby recommended it to the world's organizations.

IBM's entry into the outsourcing field eliminated any remaining stigma surrounding the concept. Other companies began to understand that outsourcing was a viable tool that they, too, could use.

# THE TRAIL TO OUTSOURCING

High profile companies, such as Digital Equipment Corporation, Andersen Consulting, AT&T Solutions and other prestigious companies followed the trails mapped out by EDS, IBM, and ADP. Outsourcing, originally viewed as a vehicle for distressed companies in need of cost reduction, became an accepted strategic tool. Senior management teams looked with new interest on this potential value driver.

## Globalization

Before IBM entered the outsourcing market, EDS had a small international operation. With the attention generated by the entry of IBM, EDS redoubled its international operations.

The French and English soon adopted outsourcing and established domestic outsourcing suppliers, such as Hoskins and the Cap Gemini Group. As outsourcing became more prominent in the U.S., European buyers became more open to embracing the trend. We now find vibrant outsourcing markets all across Europe. Asia and Australia followed, spurred by the power of multinational corporations who found it to be a useful tool.

This wave of outsourcing has been spurred on by the power of multinational corporations. Having experimented with outsourcing and finding it to be a useful tool, North American companies have exported the concept and expanded into foreign markets. Many corporations find outsourcing to be extremely helpful as they confront language, cultural and scale issues in new global markets. The multinationals have used experienced outsourcing suppliers (such as EDS, CSC, IBM and Andersen Consulting) to provide implementation on a global basis. Additionally, they have cultivated new supplier companies as a way to achieve local content requirements and avail themselves of local talent and insight. Building on these footholds, both local suppliers and major, experienced suppliers have expanded the reach of the outsourcing concept.

A good example of using local talent is the relationship between EDS and La Caixa, the largest savings bank in Europe. The Spanish financial institution, formally named Caja de Ahorros Y Pensiones de Barcelona, wanted to expand throughout Spain, opening branches everywhere.

La Caixa had 2,000 branches when it decided to use outsourcing to fuel its growth. The savings bank created three subsidiaries (a data processing business, a company to manage its telecommunications and a third to handle the support and maintenance of its desktop services through a call center), and then it outsourced its activities to those units. In 1995 EDS bought those subsidiaries, retaining all the local employees. Now the managers of the subsidiaries manage the relationship between EDS and La Caixa.

By 1999, the savings bank had more than doubled its branches to 4,200. EDS also helped the bank become a 24 x 7 financial institution. Customers can now complete financial transactions as well as buy movie passes or airline tickets at the ATM terminals that use the EDS advanced self-service technology.

# THE TRAIL TO OUTSOURCING

## New Worlds to Conquer

Once the principle of shedding the non-core process of data processing was accepted, executives began using outsourcing principles in areas outside data processing, thus giving rise to what is now known as "business process outsourcing" (BPO). Industries, such as building maintenance facilities management and vehicle maintenance and logistics, emerged as prime candidates for BPO. Organizations recognized they could get more value by outsourcing through dedicated suppliers active in these fields than by retaining these non-core processes in-house.

Successful examples of this strategy are the trucking firm Ryder (which has established Ryder Integrated Logistics, Inc.); American Airlines (which spun out its reservations department into The Sabre Group); and Exel Logistics, a warehousing logistics company. These companies quickly created a logistics outsourcing industry by leveraging their economies of scale in the purchasing of freight and warehouse space, superior process control and other key processes.

Companies like American Express (with its FDR subsidiary, which was later sold) and JCPenney Company, Inc., with its establishment of JCPenney Business Services (which has since been sold to Welsh, Carson, Anderson & Stowe and renamed as "Alliance"), went into BPO around the processing of credit cards.

Xerox entered the BPO market in reprographics. Like IBM, Xerox used its leadership position, as well as the process expertise derived from its technology base, to first define reprographics as an outsourcing niche and then to dominate that market.

The role of the Big Five accounting firms must not be underestimated when it comes to outsourcing. They offer accounting, purchasing and other BPO services.

Other industries have begun to welcome BPO. In the field of human resources, companies such as Hewitt Associates are expanding rapidly. One of Hewitt's satisfied customers is Columbia/HCA, a large healthcare provider. Columbia/HCA hired Hewitt to centralize its human resource functions. When Hewitt took over in 1997, the Columbia network included about 900 entities, each one with a few thousand employees. Hewitt created a special unit within the call center just for HC directors in the field. This unit allows them to get expedient and detailed information from representatives who have received a higher level of training.

Ross Perot set off a chain reaction when he tried to find a new way to solve a business problem. Outsourcing has proven not to be a passing fad. Instead, it has expanded from its data processing roots and now encompasses any and every business process. It has passed though the early experimentation stage and has emerged as a dependable tool.

# The Trail to Outsourcing

## The Next Frontier

The Internet stands to make the largest impact on outsourcing and will bring TINA (There Is No Alternative) to all of us. We live in a world where our cycle times are going from two months to two hours and our competitors are no longer encumbered with large bureaucracies or restricted by geography. In the face of this sea change, every company must rethink its strategies and focus on its core competencies. Companies must look at what makes them unique so they can differentiate themselves in the minds of their customers. Executives must understand how their organizations create value for their customers and then focus on those processes. This forces all organizations to divest non-core but necessary processes so they can spend their time and money on what will allow them to survive and prosper in this new world order.

Today, the hottest areas of outsourcing are Internet related. Whole new types of outsourcing are springing into existence—from purchasing portals to Application Service Providers. These newcomers stand ready to change the world forever.

## *Chapter 4*

# COMPONENTS
# OF VALUE

*"There is something which unites magic and applied science while separating both from the 'wisdom' of earlier ages. The true object is to extend Man's power to the performance of all things possible. He [Bacon] rejects magic because it does not work; but his goal is that of the magician."*
— C. S. Lewis, from *The Abolition of Man*

Gold today is a vital component of lasers and surgical instruments used to clear coronary arteries; it also is used to treat cancer and arthritis. Researchers who study DNA and cell reactions use gold, and it is used in compounds with proteins to create new lifesaving drugs. Although it is not magical, as the early alchemists believed, gold has a newly created value in the world of medicine.

Modern alchemists, still in pursuit of this wealth-generating substance, have even discovered a means of extracting it from electronics and then refining it. Minute amounts of gold are found today in computer circuit boards (and computers are in everything). A Japanese businessman has developed a technique to turn more than 10 million discarded cell phones into gold bars to be sold on the commodities markets.

The same principle works in outsourcing. A buyer extracts non-core processes from its company; and a supplier adds components (such as economies of scale and expertise) and refines them to make the buyer's company a shinier, truer substance. In so doing, new value exists in the extracted components because they can now generate wealth for both companies.

### Leverage—The Crucial Component

Adapting the meaning behind the words of the old jazz song by Dizzy Gillespie ("It don't mean a thing if it ain't got that swing") to the process of outsourcing, we can say that it don't mean a thing if it ain't got that leverage! Leverage is the key to all successful outsourcing.

For a supplier to take over an existing process and provide it back to a buyer more cheaply and at an acceptable standard of performance—and still make money—there must be a fulcrum that produces that added value. Leverage is the name we give to that fulcrum. Unfortunately, I have witnessed many companies attempting to enter the outsourcing market without acknowledging this truth—much to the dismay of their stockholders.

Leverage is a result from one or more of a number of different factors. Often, there is more than one factor working at the same time, and the most profitable outsourcing partnerships are likely to combine several for a mutually beneficial effect. Let's examine the most common leverage factors and why they work.

**The Leverage of Scale**

The use of economy of scale is a powerful source of value in business realms. The concept is simple and is comparable to water stored behind a dam. Once the dam is built, operating costs are not much greater for storing a lot of water than for storing just a little.

In outsourcing, if the supplier can transfer a buyer's process to its own operation without significantly altering the way that business function works, economies of scale may apply. If this is the case, there exists an opportunity for both supplier and buyer to benefit. If the supplier's process has under-utilized equipment or facilities, relies on computer automation, can increase purchasing power, or employ any other source of scale leverage, the parties can combine their volumes to create a significantly lower per-unit cost. This creates the potential for the buyer to enjoy lower costs while allowing the supplier to make a profit.

Examples of such use of economy of scale abound in outsourcing alliances. In the data processing field, there is data center and network management. In the logistics field, there is warehouse space, purchasing power, and the ability to share loads.

In the human resources (HR) field, there is the software used to process paychecks and administer benefits. Hewitt Associates, for example, handles all the HR needs for Southern Company, the largest producer of electricity in the United States. Southern Company's 32,000 employees, dependents, retirees and surviving spouses contact Hewitt for all questions regarding their benefits by using a toll-free number. The outsourcer is responsible for maintaining eligibility records for each employee's health and welfare plans. Hewitt also administers Southern Company's defined benefits plan.

Hewitt not only has consolidated Southern Company's benefits but also has come up with new ideas. In 1999 Hewitt allowed employees to enroll in their various plans using the Internet. In 2000, Southern Company's employees received pension estimates from the company web site. Because of its economy of scale, suppliers like Hewitt are able to provide services at a lower cost and still make adequate profits. That's because Hewitt is doing the same thing for other clients like Columbia/HCA.

Opportunities to build economies of scale in a business process are more likely to present themselves when two important conditions exist. These factors are not prerequisites for an economy of scale.

However, when they are present, there is often the potential for a supplier to move in and develop alliances with buyers, to their mutual advantage.

The first condition is that the underlying technology be mature and stable. This is particularly evident in the data processing field. The most mature data processing technology is MVS processing, which also happens to present the greatest opportunity for economies of scale; in contrast, the desktop arena is a relatively immature technology and only recently has shown any opportunity to leverage technology economies of scale.

The second condition exploiting the likelihood of economies of scale is that standardization has occurred in the business processes. Standardization is often driven through some form of government or industry regulation, as in payroll processing or banking. The maturing of the underlying technology itself can drive standardization, as in MVS processing. An emerging source of standardization is the wide acceptance of the "ERP" data processing systems that, by their nature, standardize processes such as HR, purchasing and accounting services across many companies. In so doing, they generate a potential source of economies of scale.

### The Leverage of Expertise

Another source of leverage is expertise. An outsourcing supplier must have or develop expertise superior to that of its prospective customers. Such expertise may be derived from many  sources. The supplier, for example, may have focused its full attention and investment on developing expertise in one area as its core business, while its buyers focused on a different area as their core businesses. One example of this is Andersen Consulting, which has invested hundreds of millions of dollars in becoming the world leader in application development. Although most of its buyers have developed a certain level of expertise in this area and have invested in some degree in developing their own capabilities in this area, they do not come close to Andersen Consulting's process expertise. The company has utilized its process expertise to successfully move into the business of outsourcing application development and support for many clients.

Developing or manufacturing of an underlying technology is another source of supplier expertise. This was the case with Xerox, which developed the core reprographics technology. It retains a market-leading position in the manufacturing and servicing of the equipment. Few, if any, companies can boast the in-depth process knowledge of Xerox when it comes to reprographics; consequently, the company uses this as its core point of leverage in its outsourcing business.

Due to its stock price or company brand name, a supplier may gain expertise through being positioned to attract and retain a higher level of employees. From my experience, the most notable example of a supplier using this to its leverage advantage is the relationship between Western Union and EDS.

Originally, their relationship was founded entirely on this leverage point.

Western Union was going through restructuring brought on by Chapter 11 bankruptcy and was competing for resources in a very hot New Jersey market. The company simply could not attract nor retain the technical expertise necessary to keep its computer systems running. By leveraging its acknowledged stability and trade name, EDS was able to come in as the supplier and attract high-quality employees. The employees became the resources to provide services far superior to that of the previous environment.

The expertise that provides leverage may be actual (meaning it exists in the skills and experience of the supplier's staff), or it may be ascribed (meaning it exists in the minds of those who relate to the supplier). Actual and ascribed expertise generally go together, with the former naturally leading to the latter. But ascribed expertise is an asset that can potentially be exploited without calling for much exercise of actual expertise. This can, therefore, be a significant factor in the creation of value for the supplier that is lucky enough to enjoy such status. In the examples of large and highly successful suppliers cited later in this chapter, note that a significant factor in their success was the credibility they already enjoyed because of expertise the market already ascribed to them in related areas.

Leverage through expertise can sometimes be subtle. By seriously focusing on a business process and looking at it from a new perspective, suppliers can leverage new elements. For example, at the time of this writing, a market for utility outsourcing is emerging in the United States. A utility company will contract to provide—not "power"—but a 70-degree year-round temperature for a particular office environment; it may also provide lighting year round. It has achieved some economy of scale and also may have access to less costly power than its buyers, or it may have superior purchasing power. The supplier buys the buyer's existing air conditioning and lighting equipment to accomplish the goal.

Another classic example of the leveraging of expertise now gaining market acceptance is in the healthcare field. Several suppliers of hospital equipment outsource the equipment's function, rather than sell the equipment itself. They sell their superior expertise in a technical area. They provide a service that would eliminate a hospital's need to invest in highly expensive equipment. The supplier then can turn fixed costs into variable costs, while the hospital remains current with the technology. The supplier also has access to the resale market. In effect, it will be leveraging many elements in a process—similar to the model used by Xerox when it began outsourcing its reprographics capabilities.

Hospitals are becoming increasingly computerized to improve healthcare. The Rx for a successful IT department is to outsource it. That's exactly what the University Health Network in Toronto did. It had been transferring patient charts between its three facilities via a mainframe computer. Patient Xrays, charts and lab reports were also stored in a computer database. When the hospital switched from a mainframe to a client-server system in 1995, it quickly discovered that it took a lot more resources to support its 3,000 PC workstations. The hospital also had a problem retaining talented IT staffers because the best ones always left the hospital to work for an IT company. So the Toronto hospital signed a five-year contract with Compaq to deploy 4,000 new desktops and servers as well as the required network hardware.

### The Leverage of Access

Another important leverage occurs when a supplier has access to benefits not available to its potential buyers. The things to which access may be important are many and varied. Using access to capital funds is an often-overlooked source of leverage. In the emerging utility segment of outsourcing, for example, a supplier's strategy might be to replace a buyer's existing power and lighting equipment with more efficient equipment, thus achieving cost savings. A portion of the savings could then be passed back to the buyer. An outsourcing supplier will usually be in a better position to make such a capital investment, while the buyer may not be willing or able to.

Leveraging access to lower raw material costs is another possibility. In outsourcing, this often is done through changes in geographic location (for example, by moving work to an offshore location). By taking the applications support work that used to be performed in New York City and moving it, for instance, to India or Bulgaria where the same work can be performed for a fraction of the cost, a supplier can achieve sustainable cost reductions. It may be possible for the supplier to effect a change of this nature, which is one that would be impossible for the buyer to achieve directly.

These kinds of leverage are possible due to the characteristics of a supplier's organization. These may include characteristics that it (or its parent) enjoys as an aspect of its existing business, or characteristics that it intentionally develops to improve its performance as a supplier.

But there is another kind of leverage—one that derives from combining the supplier's characteristics with the buyer's characteristics. The two organizations work together in a way that produces synergy. One example of this is a buyer that utilized its close working relationship with EDS to identify business opportunities through the EDS sales and customer network. EDS helped Neodata sign contracts to manage large customer loyalty programs, which was a new business for Neodata. The newcomer, Neodata, was able to gain the confidence of these big players through its strategic alliance with EDS. In effect, Neodata opened up a new sales channel, which proved highly profitable to it and to EDS.

**The More the Better**

A single point of leverage is often sufficient to support an outsourcing play; however, when multiple points of leverage are deployed, the opportunity for highly profitable outsourcing increases. This is illustrated through the example of payroll processing, which long has been a highly profitable outsourcing business segment. In this case, a supplier is able to leverage economy of scale derived from large data centers, centralized regulation and tax compliance, as well as common application support through the use of standard software. The supplier also derives leverage from its relative expertise in payroll processing. It also has access leverage, generated from a capital pool dedicated to investment in furthering its efficiencies.

Another example of multiple leverage points is the Application Service Providers (ASPs), one of the fastest growing areas of outsourcing as this book was going to print. An ASP makes a sizable capital investment in state-of-the-art hardware and first tier software. Companies that could never afford that kind of expenditure get to enjoy the benefits of having them by outsourcing to an ASP. The ASP creates leverage through the economies of scale created in its data centers, the need for only one Internet Service Provider, shared equipment and shared maintenance staffs. It creates process expertise leverage through its superior expertise in installing, maintaining and running the software. It creates access to capital leverage through utilizing its own capital to fund the development of its data centers.

As a result of all this leverage, companies that could never afford these software packages can now afford to take advantage of them by utilizing this new ASP vehicle. Compared with an internal function, the supplier could provide numerous advantages to the buyer.

The question now becomes: To what degree will the supplier share those advantages with the buyer, as reflected in its pricing and the quality of the services it provides? The process of agreeing on a fair price is discussed in Chapter 7.

**Examples of the Value Created by Leverage**
The value of leverage is evident in the success of some major new entrants into the outsourcing field in recent years.

*Leveraging expertise.* IBM recognized the value of its reputation—ascribed expertise in data processing and other areas—when it decided to enter the outsourcing arena. I like to refer to this concept as an organization having "market permission" to enter a new area or develop a new aspect of activity.

The success that IBM achieved by having market permission was its leverage. Big Blue's respect, credibility and trust were its leverage. There was an implicit promise that IBM as an outsourcing supplier could do what it said it could. Since then, IBM has gone from strength to strength, based on its reputation and the enormous amount of successful outsourcing relationships it has established with many companies.

Xerox also leveraged the value of its established reputation. Additionally, it leveraged its expertise and ownership of the reprographics process and manufacturing capabilities.

AT&T Solutions was able to enter a highly competitive field (even though that field was dominated at the time by EDS and IBM) and quickly establish market leadership by leveraging its undisputed credibility. It also leveraged its ability to deliver telecommunications services. AT&T's advantage was in being a major telecommunications carrier with access to world-class expertise. IBM, Xerox and AT&T each created billion-dollar outsourcing supplier businesses in a short period of time, adding significantly to their valuations.

Ownership of software or a proprietary software capability is another example of a company having market permission to enter into outsourcing. Pittsburgh's Mellon Bank Corporation developed a stable and successful banking product and then leveraged that software capability to other smaller banks that did not want to pay for such capability. At the heart of JCPenney's leverage when it launched its credit card processing business was its ownership of proprietary credit card processing software, along with its core centers and sorting equipment. The true star of this genre is American Airlines, which took its impressive airline reservation, ticketing and operations software capabilities and created a standalone subsidiary – The Sabre Group—and outsourced Sabre's capabilities to other airlines. (Sabre has since become a spinout.)

*Leveraging expertise with brand-name awareness.* Andersen Consulting is a classic example of a company leveraging its applications outsourcing practice. Despite its early and unsuccessful forays into data processing, Andersen eventually fell back on its true competence—its ability to develop and maintain applications—and has since moved to the forefront. It is now a market leader in that outsourcing niche.

Ryder used its brand-name awareness in the trucking industry, combined with its logistics expertise, when it created its logistics outsourcing supplier company.

Many of the Big Five accounting firms are now entering the BPO marketplace. Perhaps the most aggressive and the best organized of them is PwC. These firms leverage their substantial customer network in combination with superior reengineering capability and process knowledge in order to create new outsourcing opportunities in accounting and purchasing.

*Leveraging scale.* The Royal Dutch/Shell Group of Companies realized that it was spending well over a billion dollars a year worldwide on IT and other administrative services. Confronting ongoing efforts to refocus its business, it faced the issue of whether to divest itself of non-core processes through an outsourcing strategy or to create an outsourcing supplier firm. It did the latter. One of the benefits of being a huge multinational company is that scale is its birthright. Shell used its birthright in creating the new company.

The idea was the brainchild of Phil Carroll, the president of Shell U.S. at the time the process began. Shell's corporate culture is one of thought leadership, and they truly thought about what they were trying to accomplish. Shell had achieved a leading position in the oil industry by adopting strategic thinking and making it work. What they did with the outsourcing concept is another reflection of such leadership.

Shell chose a variety of services—facilities management, accounting, IT, data center, desktop, network, applications support, application development, purchasing—and spun them out into a new company. The new group was to think and behave like an outsourcing supplier—handling all the spun-out processes for its parent company as well as for other companies.

It wasn't easy for the new company to treat its parent company as an outside entity—basically, to be a part of the parent company, yet not a part of it. Originally trained to think like an internal agency of the parent company, the new company's staff found itself in an arms-length relationship with its parent. It was difficult at first to understand the special nature of the outsourcing market interface. There were numerous issues that had to be worked out on both sides—the issue of measurement, how to define value, the right to make (or not to make) a profit, and how to compensate staff in the new company. They also had to figure out how to develop a professional sales force to sell the new company's supplier services to companies other than its Shell parent. Gradually, Shell International has been resolving these issues and is growing. It has some external business and some internal business in an arms-length manner.

Shell's concept in creating the new company was to run the spun-out service areas as a business. It has capitalized on the key issues of scale, leverage and core competency. The creation of the new company freed the other operating companies within The Royal Dutch/Shell Group of companies to focus on their own core competencies.

Shell then recognized that it had neither the expertise nor the inclination to deal with facilities management. So it spun off that subsidiary into a joint venture with The Intellisource Group, a company whose outsourcing expertise also includes auditing and accounting; technical graphics and publishing; mail services; human resources; communications; telecommunications; purchasing; IT, travel and transportation; duplication services; library services; and forms and records management. Shell sealed its joint venture deal with an equity position in Intellisource. The entire process clearly evidences the thought leadership of Shell's management. The outsourcing supplier created by Shell now sells an array of services to the rest of the petrochemical industry, as well as to its sister Shell operating companies.

Perhaps the most daring move in leveraging scale took place when General Motors bought EDS, taking a billion-dollar company and adding over $4 billion to it, which raised the company's market valuation significantly. As U.S. Senator Everett Dirksen is said to have remarked, a billion here, a billion there, and pretty soon you're talking about real money.

### The Buyer's Perspective in Recognizing Value

So far, most of my comments and examples have illustrated the fact that outsourcing suppliers create value in several ways. Equally important to the process is the buyer's recognition that it should never enter into an outsourcing relationship unless it is clear that value is present. Moreover, neither party should undergo the painful steps of first exploring the potential of outsourcing or the traumatic transfer of ownership of the process, with all the risk and dislocation that entails, without value having been determined on both sides.

Several points of leverage also appear on the buyer's side of the ledger. Flexible pricing or the ability to scale easily is one of these. In many outsourcing relationships, the benefit the buyer receives is that it can match its consumption of resources with its use of the resources.

An example of this is Halliburton Company, which outsourced its HR and benefits administration function. The company specialized in managing larger construction projects throughout the world and was faced with significant swings in the number of employees. One of its many business challenges was to be able to mobilize quickly—to add or subtract staff on short notice. This requirement meant that an overly large HR and benefits department had to be maintained at all times. By outsourcing this function, the company was able to match its HR cost to its business cycle, thereby saving a substantial amount of money.

This kind of buyer leverage is particularly likely to be in the cards if the supplier utilizes economies of scale as its key leverage point. In such instances, the buyer's alternative—of sustaining its own internal infrastructure—is unlikely to be able to compete with what the supplier can offer. The fixed nature of the infrastructure makes it difficult to reduce cost in bad times or to scale up to meet increased usage in good times. Such pricing flexibility obtained through outsourcing can be a very powerful benefit for the buyer.

Another buyer value is lower investment intensity. Through outsourcing, a buyer can avoid investments in internal infrastructure it would otherwise be forced to make if it continued to control the process internally. As investment dollars become scarce and are needed for core processes, being able to avoid the need for such ongoing investments is a clear benefit to a buyer.

Increased management focus is an important leverage point for the buyer. By ridding itself of the responsibility to run and manage the outsourced process, a management team can free time and energy to focus on a company's core processes. After all, these are what define the buyer in the marketplace where it competes. In a world where managers are faced with increasing demands on their time, freedom from the decision making and analysis that would have been involved in a now-outsourced process can be of significant benefit to a buyer.

### How Can a Buyer Apply Leverage?

The first step is to recognize what kinds of leverage are available from the supplier community. Interestingly enough, not all suppliers are created equal in applying leverage, from a buyer's perspective. Each potential supplier has different capabilities and strengths. A word of warning here: just because a supplier has access to a point of leverage does not mean that it will be willing to utilize it for a particular transaction in such a way that will significantly share the benefit with the buyer. In general, however, suppliers are in the business of utilizing their leverage and, in a competitive situation, they can be expected to share some benefits with their buyers.

The first consideration for a potential supplier and potential buyer is to identify sufficient potential sources of leverage that will allow the provision of quality services at a relative cost advantage. This is what will become the value to both parties.

Many companies that have aspired to become outsourcing suppliers find it extremely difficult to come to grips with the fact that good intentions and deep pockets are not enough to ensure success in the outsourcing field. Often, their senior executives lack a clear vision of the need for leverage or a clear plan for how to build it. Without leverage, outsourcing makes no sense. There can be no cost advantage without it. Eventually both the supplier and the buyer suffer without it.

The key to success is to understand the leverage in the relationship. The more leverage there is, the more opportunity the supplier will have for cost-effective pricing; and the more chance there will be for an outsourcing arrangement to produce the ongoing flow of value.

A buyer should also have a clear idea of how it expects a supplier to generate and sustain leverage. Buyers don't want to end up like Alice in Lewis Carroll's *Alice in Wonderland*, who asked the Cheshire Cat: "Would you tell me, please, which way I ought to go from here?"

" That depends a good deal on where you want to get to," said the Cat.

" I don't much care where," said Alice.

"Then it doesn't matter which way you go," said the Cat.

"So long as I get somewhere," Alice added.

"Oh, you're sure to do that," said the Cat, "if you only walk long enough."

Similarly, a buyer without a clear vision of what is being leveraged is in for a very long and pointless walk.

Once a clear picture of the potential leverage points has emerged, the buyer should consider the sustainability of the point of leverage. In contracting, a short-term advantage may be all that is needed. Outsourcing, however, should be for the long term; so the leverage on which it is based should also be sustainable over the long term. If the leverage is a one-time occurrence, the buyer is more likely to have problems in the latter years of the contract.

The buyer should not interfere with the supplier's leverage by failing to give the supplier sufficient scope within which to bring its economies of scale and process expertise to bear. The buyer needs to be very clear about what it wants from the relationship. Remember the refrain from the country/western song: "Younger women, older whiskey, faster horses and more money?" What the buyer seeks in an outsourcing relationship is similar: reduced bottom-line costs, improved quality, improved cycle time, better use of management's time, and increased focus on core competency. Good use of leverage gives these benefits to the buyer.

Restricting the supplier's ability to deploy its leverage assets will interfere with the buyer's benefits. If leverage is deployed successfully, the result should be lower cost, higher quality services and flexible pricing. Many, if not most, outsourcing relationships are initiated for only one reason—the buyer believes that it can receive a substantial cost reduction by outsourcing. There is nothing to be ashamed about in this analysis; in many instances, substantial cost savings are delivered.

In one outsourcing contract that I helped structure, the cost of the contract to the buyer was approximately $120 million. The client calculated that the value produced (the estimated savings to the buyer on a net present-value basis) was in excess of $100 million. In this particular instance, the supplier utilized economies of scale in its data centers and its superior process expertise to generate enough leverage to provide this savings back to the buyer and still make a fair profit. This is an exceptional situation, and this level of savings is unlikely to be available to most buyers. It certainly proves, though, that outsourcing can generate significant returns. It is a classic example of outsourcing's ability to transform a mundane process into gold.

*Part*
# TWO

---

## PRINCIPLES IN ACTION

# Chapter 5

# FINDING THE
# RIGHT FORMULA

*"If I have seen further than others, it is by standing
upon the shoulders of giants."*
—Isaac Newton

*"We are now uniquely privileged to sit side by side
with the giants on whose
shoulders we stand.*
—Gerald Holton

The fact that the European alchemists of the
Middle Ages carried out experiment after experiment was no guarantee for success. Many of them
worked from notebooks compiled by their predeces-
sors. Known as "books of spells," they were full of
details about separating and distilling elements and
then uniting them in another form. But they also
were full of secret codes and riddles, as the process

of turning lead into gold was not intended for everyone to learn.

Although leverage is essential in creating value in outsourcing, it is not sufficient unto itself. As many of the examples in this book illustrate, a lasting relationship demands that the advantages produced by the leverage be shared equitably between supplier and buyer, rather than being allowed to accrue for the benefit of only—or even primarily—one party. An outsourcing arrangement that produces profit for either the supplier or the buyer in a severely lopsided way is doomed to be short lived.

Some of the early alchemists risked life and limb experimenting with explosive mixtures in their quest to turn lead into gold. In a similar way, there have been many unsuccessful attempts at outsourcing, as the early practitioners experimented to find the right formula to generate value. Suppliers have lost money before they found out about the need for leverage or because they overestimated the leverage available. Buyers have failed to save money or improve their process by not recognizing how to exploit their suppliers' leverage. Buyers have failed to negotiate their fair share of the gold or allow themselves to be taken advantage of as the contract progressed.

The material which follows in this and subsequent chapters serves as a guide for buyers and suppliers in developing agreements that ensure that value is shared in fair and reasonable proportions; that the arrangement is a mutually beneficial one; and that the contract is structured to ensure their commitment to working together and is flexible enough to make adjustments over the years. An outsourcing relationship works much like a good marriage.

**Pressure on the Container**

In my observation, a disturbingly large portion of relationships between outsourcing suppliers and buyers unfortunately develops a significant adversarial component. On the surface, this should be deeply disturbing to both buyer and supplier; however, when the elements that drive such a conflict are understood, it can also produce benefits for both parties. These adversarial components are the supplier's requirement to increase revenues, the buyer's requirement to increase profits, rapidly changing technologies (particularly in high-tech), and the fact that business objectives are subject to rapid change.

Think of an outsourcing contract as being like a container. As the adversarial components operate, they introduce additional pressure into that container as time goes by. Notice that the pressure comes from both the supplier's side and the buyer's side.

Every supplier has an obligation to its stockholders to grow revenue and increase profit. Suppliers also must face the fact that the technical nature of the service or commodity being outsourced changes over time. For example, the fundamental nature of desktop services constantly changes. While the speed of change may differ among services, the fact of change itself is a constant. An example of a buyer's

# The Problem with Managing Outsourcing

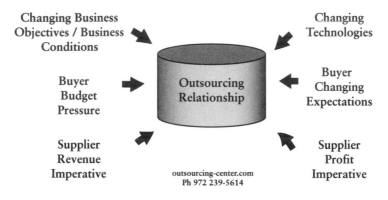

business objective is the reduction of cycle time from order to shipment. Such change may be driven by competition, by regulation and by other economic factors. These contrast with pressures on the supplier's side and put pressure on the container (the contract) all the time.

Since these pressures are inherent and inevitable in our business world, we must make containers out of the strongest materials, designing them to withstand pressure as much as possible. We must build in a safety valve that can be used to relieve pressure when it occurs—in order to avoid an explosion that would blow the thing to smithereens! We must also seek ways to reduce those external and internal pressures as much as possible.

Translating the container analogy into the language of outsourcing, this means the buyer and seller must do six things: 1) Clearly define the scope and elements of the processes to be supplied, including distinguishing between those that are central to it and those that are ancillary or added contributions; 2) Agree on an appropriate price for each aspect of what is being supplied; 3) Provide for flexibility as circumstances and requirements change; 4) Make a relatively short-term contract with provision for multiple extensions and renegotiations, rather than a single, unvarying long-term contract; 5) Work to establish a spirit of alliance based on the alignment of motivation and objectives; and 6) Provide a suitable means of measuring performance for each aspect of the agreement. (This last item is so important that I have devoted the next chapter to the measurement of performance.)

## Five Steps to Eliminate Pressure

You can build a well-designed, titanium container with a pressure valve in five steps.

***Step 1: Defining the elements (scope) of the outsourced process.*** Defining the elements of the outsourced process and the metrics used to measure them, together with constructing an adequate contract, all work together in creating a titanium container.

Historically, suppliers have intentionally tried to introduce a great deal of mystery into the outsourcing process. To demystify the process, a buyer must first break down its relationship with the supplier in terms of the actual services being provided.

As obvious as the need for this requirement is, I have found that few buyers take the time to adequately define what it is they are buying. What usually happens is that the procurement process focuses on getting what is perceived as a good price, leaving the definition of the scope of the services for the supplier to establish after the buyer has retained the supplier. In these cases the supplier determines during the course of the agreement what it will and won't do. If you are a buyer who does this, you will be playing the game on a steep slope. Even worse, you will have to play uphill. A more prudent approach is to establish the scope of the services before going to the market with a Request for Proposal (RFP) or approaching a supplier.

Start the process by defining what contributions you need from the supplier. When assessing value, you must understand what is valuable to you. All buyers agree that low costs are good; beyond that, they vary widely when defining value. Some firms may need to bring on a new software application quickly while others can wait. Some customers just need to have access to their computers 99 percent of the time. This is adequate for most companies. But an on-line brokerage firm can never be down. It needs to be up 99.999999 percent of the time, and this seemingly small difference in performance adds a huge amount of cost to the service. That's why it is so crucial to determine what is important.

# Finding the Right Formula

In further defining the process, consider the scope. Scope describes the boundaries of the process so both parties can see clearly where one responsibility ends and the other begins. For example, in logistics, one might choose to break apart the transportation from the warehousing, and the inbound logistics from the outbound logistics. As another example, in back-office outsourcing, the agreement might include such services as internal audit, central accounting, Securities and Exchange Commission reporting, divisional accounting and analysis. In an HR example, the services could be broken down into payroll; benefits administration; relocation services and policy development and administration.

There are two traps in trying to define the process. The first and most common is to conclude that an outsourced business function, such as telecommunications, is a homogenous service and that one set of definitions and metrics will suffice. Often, this is not the case. For example, the telecommunications process is made up of several related components. The problem with defining them all at the same time is that there can be a great temptation to take shortcuts with the definition process. The significant effort required to define the process is painful and expensive, but the discipline of breaking up the service into its constituent parts is worth the effort. Furthermore, it is also extremely helpful for those individuals who have to administer the relationship. Because it provides a clear and easy way to administrate process boundary, it enables both parties to determine what services are in and out of scope.

The second and more significant reason to break up the services into homogenous components is that the different components are usually cost drivers that are based on different technologies; this causes the drivers to be influenced by different business issues and change at a different pace.

In the case of telecommunications, it is helpful to divide it into at least two different service areas— transportation (the dial tone and the moving of voice and data across a telephone line) and management of the network (this includes network design, routine maintenance and trouble shooting.) In many parts of the world, the transportation segment is a commodity that is under intense competition. This leads to continual price reductions.

Historically, it has been unwise to bundle transport with the customized and more stable management service because it then becomes extremely difficult for both the supplier and buyer to equitably divide the ever-falling transport/shipping costs. Where these services have been combined, my experience is that either the buyer or supplier ends up feeling taken advantage of. This can lead to confrontation and, often, to contractual problems for both parties.

The best example of the need to unbundle is the rise of the Internet. If a buyer tells a network manager how to manage the network, those dictates do not allow the supplier to take advantage of any new technology that comes along. Using old technology typically leads to higher cost and poor service. The supplier would not be able to introduce the Internet technology to the buyer unless it had the freedom to make these decisions.

The second trap—breaking up the process first—is the flip side of the trap of concluding that one set of metrics and definitions will suffice. This can make the elements too granular. The problem with this approach is that the buyer ends up telling the supplier how to run the process. This is also a major source of loss of leverage and value.

The solution to these traps, then, is to define the services in such a way that there is a homogenous similarity. This often will occur where the same technologies are in use and the same business interests are being served. Where this is not the case, a wise buyer or supplier will at least pause to consider whether or not a further decomposition would be helpful. It's often not easy to distinguish between homogenous groups, and it's certainly worth getting expert advice from a knowledgeable outsider like the Everest Group.

In every outsourcing relationship, buyers and sellers must specify exactly what services are being purchased. Often the buyer has unwritten expectations that the supplier make additional contributions to the buyer's business goals. Sometimes the buyer expects continuous improvement where none is explicitly defined or measured. Just as often, a buyer expects that a supplier will leverage its capabilities in other areas to assist the buyer in its struggle to compete. If these benefits are anticipated, they should be defined and measured. When such aspirations defy definition and objective metrics, they are unlikely to occur or are unrealistic expectations.

Buyers need to realize that it is unfair for suppliers to have to agree on a price until they understand what they will be providing and how it will be measured.

*Step 2: Agreeing on an appropriate price.* Agreeing on a fair price is usually the focus of the slow mating dance referred to as the request for proposal (RFP) and negotiation process. Although establishing a fair and advantageous price is extremely important, it is neither as easy nor as sustainable as it might at first appear. (I will address this topic more in Chapter 7).

The most common trap that a buyer can fall into is to negotiate a price before it has adequately defined the services and agreed with the supplier about the degrees of accountability that the supplier will undertake in providing those services. In such an instance, the buyer finds that it has no meaningful price for what it has bought. Either the services will be changed to meet the supplier price, or new charges will be added over time to compensate the supplier. Sometimes this phenomenon works against the supplier, and it loses money (or, at least, does not make the kind of profits it anticipated when it agreed on the price). Whatever the situation is, the solution is clear. The parties must make sure the services and metrics are defined and agreed upon before price negotiations take place.

Before embarking on an expensive RFP process, both buyers and suppliers need to remember that in a free market, price is a function of competition and negotiating prowess—it is not a function of fairness, justice, or supplier leverage (such as economies of scale). If there is only one supplier, the buyer is at a strong disadvantage. Furthermore, for a buyer who wants a competitive market price, it is imperative that there still be competition when price is negotiated at the end of the RFP process. Buyers often rush to eliminate competition and only negotiate with a single supplier. Interestingly, this truth is seldom lost on suppliers. They understand the benefit of a sole bid opportunity or being the only party left at the negotiating table. Many suppliers have developed elaborate sales methodologies to try to ensure just these conditions. (New suppliers, of course, may wish to study these techniques.)

This same truth also extends into the relationship once it has been consummated. In this instance, it is often a function of the relationship that the buyer must purchase the new services from the incumbent supplier. The problem occurs whenever the buyer wants to change what it is buying or add new services to the offering. The buyer can control this one-sided negotiating position somewhat by establishing predetermined pricing for new services. However, this action has significant limitations, since the areas that pose the most problems to the buyer are new services or changes to existing services that were not, nor could have been, anticipated. It is for this reason that the buyer is well advised not to sign contracts that are longer than the natural time it takes to amortize the supplier's investment to get into the relationship. Correspondingly, this is a major reason why suppliers expend so much time and money convincing their prospective customers to sign 10-year agreements.

Both the buyer and supplier should avoid building in a premium on a service, anticipating that it would compensate the supplier to perform above and beyond the call of duty. What inevitably happens is that the supplier comes to believe that an extra premium is its right and due; the supplier does not view it as an incentive to add new services nor to perform any better than it otherwise would do. It is far better for both parties to compensate the supplier fairly at the market rate and for the buyer to pay for extra services when it needs them. In this way, the supplier has the necessary incentive to react with enthusiasm and speed to new service requests. The alternative is a continual low-grade warfare in which the buyer demands new services that it believes it has paid for, and the supplier drags its feet in the hope that it will be compensated for providing services beyond its current pricing structure.

***Step 3: Providing for flexibility.*** Achieving flexibility in outsourcing relationships looks to become the Holy Grail of the industry for the foreseeable future. In my comparison of outsourcing to a container, a safety valve is a necessary feature to release pressure from the container. In outsourcing, any safety valve is something that adds flexibility to the relationship. The need for flexibility in a long-term relationship is obvious; technologies, business conditions, business objectives and personnel all change at a rapid pace. Outsourcing relationships must adapt to some extent, or there will be open warfare between the parties.

The problem is that outsourcing is inherently inflexible, as the container illustration demonstrates. Basically, an outsourcing relationship is a vehicle for change in which the buyer asks the supplier to provide lower costs or increased functionality (sometimes both concurrently). In almost every case, the supplier has some up-front investment it must make to achieve the goals, and it expects to amortize that investment over the life of the contract. This investment, combined with enhanced negotiating power due to lack of competition, makes the supplier relatively unwilling to make changes to the environment without receiving a healthy reward.

The supplier is in a relatively strong bargaining position because it is often the only entity that understands what is required to change the buyer's infrastructure or processes. Not surprisingly, this can result in a supplier charging relatively high rates for execution of trivial tasks. Some of the changes that a buyer must make may not be in the supplier's interest, particularly when the supplier must reduce its costs to meet new business challenges. A common scenario would be a reduction in staff leading to a lower demand for the outsourced service.

Once we represented a buyer who wanted to move many of its order functions to the Internet to become more competitive in today's connected world. Its supplier had to write an interface to the front end of the order entry and pricing programs under its control so this customer could migrate to the Net. The supplier charged a high premium to prepare this interface. The buyer felt frustrated and abused, believing the price was too high for the work involved.

Another change requiring flexibility is one that typically occurs when a company moves to a new area of technology—such as client/server to reduce the workload on the mainframe (one of a supplier's most profitable services). Sometimes the supplier refuses to assist with the conversion or work to ensure that the new client/server systems can interface with the mainframe system.

In one such case, a supplier was asked to provide an extract of the data that was stored on the mainframe. It did so, but it put the data out in a format that was difficult to access by the new client/server environment. Coincidentally, it ensured that the buyer would have to pay additional costs, and the supplier had established predetermined pricing for new services.

The speed at which technology is changing requires flexibility. One example of this is the often-outsourced service of desktop support. The rate of change in this business is mind-blowing. As I travel worldwide, I consistently ask people if they have any idea what a desktop will look like in 10 years—or even five years. The answer overwhelmingly is "no"—they have no idea. It is, therefore, ludicrous to try to build a contract where pricing and performance for desktop services is predicted five or 10 years into the future. The rate of technology change alone dictates that this is profoundly unwise; nevertheless, companies do it. Many buyers today rush headlong into such arrangements, but these contracts always favor suppliers.

Although it is impossible to solve completely the flexibility problem, breaking a relationship into its homogenous services and having separate service agreements with adequate definitions is very important. This adds flexibility to the relationship because small adjustments can be made to specific services without having to renegotiate the entire contract. Furthermore, there is more clarity and focus on the services, allowing for an easier change control mechanism.

Buyers should avoid "bundling" services and cross-subsidizing services whenever possible; this only leads to supplier inflexibility. The unnecessary interrelationships brought about from this practice make it very difficult for the supplier to deal honestly and straightforwardly with any changes that may be necessary. Some suppliers intentionally bundle their services, hoping they can command higher prices, rather than having to expose the various components that can then be benchmarked more easily. While this practice may work for a while, my experience has been that the buyer will eventually catch on and then become resentful. Bundling and its effect on pricing will be more fully discussed in Chapter 7.

There are two major ways to add flexibility into the contract to allow for adjustments. First, the buyer can be prepared to allow the supplier to add new services to the relationship and to use the potential for that new revenue to bargain for meaningful changes to existing services. Almost every supplier seeks to expand its outsourcing relationships, and the prospect of new business is a powerful tool in the hands of the buyer. Interestingly, most buyers forfeit this tool by giving their suppliers new business without using it as a vehicle to drive change.

Second, business-oriented incentives can be developed to provide the supplier with an economic incentive to make contributions to the buyer's business objectives outside the contract. Incentives act to change the nature of the relationship and allow the supplier to make higher profits while, at the same time, adding to the total value. In relationships where these incentives are in place, the supplier typically is more flexible in adjusting the core services to the needs of the buyer because it has far more than just one portion of revenue at stake. Incentives are powerful tools, and examples of their use are given later in this chapter. How to pay for these value-added components is covered in Chapter 7.

# FINDING THE RIGHT FORMULA

An excellent example of a flexible outsourcing relationship exists between Microsoft Corporation and ENTEX Information Services. Microsoft, widely touted as a visionary giant in the marketplace, sought an outsourcing relationship that meshed with its philosophy. That search led to ENTEX, a company much like Microsoft. Mark Achzenick, Microsoft vendor account manager, states that ENTEX is aggressive in its core competencies, keeping the company at the top of the industry and out in front. According to Achzenick, the key issue for Microsoft is that ENTEX is flexible. The company works its buyers on modeling the services it wants to perform and enjoys stepping "out of the box."

Their relationship is twofold. ENTEX is the service provider for Microsoft's help desk services for employees using the company's products within the Microsoft environment, and it performs desk-side repair activity. It is also a business partner, reselling Microsoft services.

Everything is service-level driven. ENTEX owns the process, from the call origination to final resolution. The call center is located in a building near the Microsoft corporate campus in Redmond, Washington; other services are located onsite at Microsoft. Because Microsoft, prior to the ENTEX agreement, was operating what Achzenick calls "a body-shop service" (with multiple suppliers supervised by company personnel) the software company had a few individuals in management at those areas. Because of the talent base at ENTEX, Microsoft began to utilize that management staff elsewhere in its company to perform core functions. ENTEX brought in service talent to fill those gaps.

Microsoft, as the developer of the Windows operating system, has a complex environment that supports more than release-type operating systems. This means that it must be extremely flexible and in tune with a buyer's internal initiatives. Microsoft needs to be prepared to support beta products (those not yet fully released to market) on the desktop long before any other supplier and before a training program exists. This is an example of something that may deviate from a standard help desk and desk-side support organization.

This outsourcing alliance not only frees Microsoft from delivery of these services, but it also provides other benefits. It enables the buyer to deal with the help desk from a business perspective (versus managing head count), and it offers better career paths for service technicians. Driving the business from the supplier's service-level perspective allows Microsoft to focus on the delivery of its core services to its end users.

The fact that ENTEX is a reseller means that it is tied into the Original Equipment Manufacturer (OEM) channel with Compaq Computer Corporation, Toshiba Corporation, Gateway and other OEMs. That experience is invaluable in the generation of ideas for the future, and Microsoft relies heavily on ENTEX in those areas to make sure that best practices are used within Microsoft's environment and that service support is done in a very innovative fashion. In some cases, that can lead to working with ENTEX on a new way to deliver a service level agreement (SLA) measurement, which has not been done before. (Service level agreements are fully discussed in Chapter 6.) This is, again, where flexibility comes back into play.

***Step 4: Making the contract short term and flexible.*** Going back to the container analogy, no container (or contract)—not even one made of titanium—can withstand a constant increase in pressure. Without a safety valve permitting the pressure to escape, it will turn inward and become destructive. Similarly, the constant push and pull on the contract will cause pressure that becomes a source of acrimony or conflict between supplier and buyer. To have real flexibility in an outsourcing relationship, the contract length for each service area cannot be too long. While the relationship can, and should be, a long one, the length of the contract itself must match the service that it covers.

The solution is to provide a systematic way to release pressure by shortening the length of the contract. In recent years, most companies and consultants have tried to make stronger contracts that favor buyers more than traditional outsourcing deals. It makes sense that 10-year contracts will have more problems in their latter years than three-year contracts, because a container that only has to last three years has a much better chance of retaining its shape and purpose. Many companies now understand this and structure shorter contracts.

Suppliers, however, do not see shorter contracts as an automatic solution to buyer/supplier strife. Suppliers offer a laundry list of reasons for wanting longer contracts. They begin with the fact that backlog is a factor in how their corporate stock is valued. They also cite the expense of entering into a contract in the first place. Suppliers have a vested interest in trying to make the contract as long as possible. They want to amortize the transition cost over a longer period, and they want to avoid the business dislocation that comes from having to renegotiate. And, suppliers historically have achieved much higher profit margins in the latter part of their contracts. Shorter contracts tend to eliminate some of these profits.

In England, there is a saying that "different horses are better for different courses." This applies to outsourcing as well as to horse racing. Different outsourcing services can have different termination lengths. For example, when a buyer outsources facilities management for a building, the basic technology change is the staff. Furthermore, the business objectives pertaining to location tend to be less ephemeral. This allows for a relatively long contract. There is still the underlying need for the supplier to increase profits and revenues. Business conditions and technology still change. No outsourcing contract should last forever.

Switching costs is an incentive to both parties to sustain long-term relationships that endure through changes in business conditions, technology shifts, and management turnover.

Dislocation and business interruption costs are another incentive for long-term relationships. Any significant transfer of a process to a third party will cause employee insecurity and dislocation. As Machiavelli advised, "There is nothing more difficult, nothing more dangerous than to introduce a new order of things."

At its heart, outsourcing is a new order of things. So it is naive to believe that a transfer of funds, people, and work outside of a company will not cause significant angst and resistance from the internal staff. Some fight the process because it represents a loss of power, budget and prestige. Others feel it is a betrayal of the employees who are being transferred out of the company or who lose their jobs. Others react purely out of pride and claim that no other company could possibly do the job as well. There will be some dislocation, and it will affect the buyer's ongoing business process. Dislocation carries with it a high cost that is difficult to measure. Anyone who has been through one of these gut-wrenching transfers will tell you that they are in no hurry to repeat the experience.

High transaction costs also make long-term relationships sensible. Almost all outsourcing transactions are complex, often requiring significant investments in management time, consulting, and legal fees for the buyer. The process is also expensive for the supplier. The cost of sales on a bid can often run well over $200,000 and, for the mega deals of a billion dollars, costs can run into the millions. These costs grow in importance when you consider that the average supplier's "bid-to win-ratio" is one win per six bids. In short, the transaction costs are high for both sides.

Often, a supplier must make a major investment to transfer the workload from the buyer's infrastructure to its own. Usually, this cost is buried in the supplier's pricing. Then there are the costs of no-longer-needed existing infrastructure. These are dealt with either by accounting adjustments, sale of equipment, or having the supplier finance it and charge for it over time.

Almost all outsourcing relationships involve a significant investment by the supplier in the form of reengineering the business process to drive out cost and improve quality. The sizes of these investments will vary with the complexity of the process, the size of the infrastructure and the quality of the existing process to be reengineered. These investments can be substantial, yet not always obvious to the buyer.

One common but often overlooked component of this investment is the cost to install and implement the account management team. The cost of implementing the supplier's management team is often recognized, but many buyers overlook the cost of their own relationship management team and the investment in tools and training needed to manage the relationship. Suppliers understand that profit margins are much larger in the latter part of a contract, particularly in a longer one; but counteracting this profit margin is the high cost of getting into the relationship because of its substantial investment in taking over the buyer's processes.

These, then, are the countervailing pressures that push the parties into a longer-term relationship. Defining this balance is critical. I believe in long-term relationships and short-term contracts. There is no need to change suppliers at the end of the contract; the need, instead, is to dissolve the container (contract) and build a new one. In the case of desktop, for example, three years might be the appropriate timeframe. At the end of the second year, desktop, technology and business objectives usually have changed to such a degree that the underlying assumptions have caused the container to split at the seams. In the case of a three-year contract, the buyer can negotiate new process boundaries and pricing after two years, knowing that the supplier understands that, if they cannot come to terms that are close to market, the buyer will place the process out to bid over the next year.

A short-term contract allows a buyer to renegotiate in good faith with its supplier, with the legitimate threat that it may switch suppliers. The buyer does not have to replace the supplier, but introducing the legitimate threat of competition raises the stakes and allows both sides to examine their options. This usually yields a marked increase in supplier flexibility.

***Step 5: Aligning motivations and objectives.*** The most successful outsourcing relationships occur when the buyer and the supplier find ways to align their company's interests and management team's motivations. As we have seen in the container analogy, natural forces, such as profit and revenue growth, drive the two parties apart. These forces, however, can be overcome and even produce highly successful, long-term relationships.

To return to the container analogy, it's helpful to understand that pressure in and of itself is benign. For instance, water pressure can be put to productive or nonproductive uses. Water pressure in a flooded river is destructive, eroding the riverbanks, posing danger to people and destroying property. However, when water pressure is used to turn a turbine, create electric power and drive water mills, it is used for beneficial purposes. In the outsourcing industry, we educate both buyers and suppliers in how to structure the performance of these relationships for a more equal balance.

Pressure relief can be achieved through the creation of metrics, or by directing the supplier to assist in achieving business objectives, and then developing a series of targets and metrics to measure consequences. As the supplier deploys its energies to meet the targets, it creates value that becomes the basis for growing revenue and/or growing profit in a win-win way (rather than at the buyer's expense). In other words, the supplier creates value and reaps some of that value.

This, then, is the two-step solution to having a contract/container that retains its shape and performs as expected. By combining short-term contracts and re-channeling energy to productive uses, a basis is built for win-win relationships that last beyond contract length. This process creates self-sustaining value—and that, after all, is what those who outsource seek to achieve.

**Three Case Studies**

What follows are three case studies of aligning motivation. The suppliers in these instances were given incentives to develop something new, which worked to the advantage of both parties. Even if the buyer does not choose to reward the supplier for achieving a business objective (which I think is a mistake), having tangible "stretch" goals (such as those exhibited in these three examples) can transform the nature of the relationship and focus both parties on a higher level of achievement.

*Case Study 1: How a $500,000 investment saved millions.* This is the story of how an insurance company with a clear business objective used outsourcing to create value. This client, who requested anonymity, wanted to reduce its claims-processing expense and also cut the cycle time for processing claims. The ability to make payments quickly can be a strategic advantage in terms of selling quality insurance to customers, and the company decided that it wanted to compete along those lines. So there were two interlinked objectives—to cut the cost by

10 percent and to reduce cycle time from 45 to three days.

To understand this scenario, you must understand that health claims processing systems reside on mainframe ("legacy") computers. These are long-term systems with a lot of money invested in them, and it would cost a lot of money and time to replace them. The cost of replacing the one this company had would have exceeded $100 million. Overhauling the application that ran claims processing was not something to be done casually.

Over the years, the company had put all kinds of checks and balances into its systems to check for abuse or fraud. The process that took place would throw claims out to a person to examine; that person would then consult the policy book to see how to respond. As a result of this process, the company resembled a ship with a hold full of clerks chained to their oars in the claims-processing galley, waiting for the system to spit out exceptions. Almost everything eventually hit at least one exception because the system was so complex.

One solution was to redevelop the system, inputting new rules into it; but that would have been a very expensive, long, drawn-out process. The company faced the challenge of wanting to make an immediate impact; but this translated into cutting back on the number of clerks and cutting down the processing time. The company did not want to eliminate some clerks, and it wanted to give them more productive things to do.

The decision made was to create a joint effort, whereby the supplier would buy a workstation-based, off-the-shelf, desktop managed, expert system package. The supplier loaded the new rules into it. It put in a program so that the buyer electronically could pull information out of the mainframe system (basically tricking the system into thinking an operator did this). The new system would go through and query every transaction; determine where the claim had been put on hold; then read and execute the instructions of the policy manual. Using the new workstations, the company was able to push transactions through the system very quickly. This software-based system accomplished the buyer's goals. It replaced a crew of clerks and compressed cycle time from 45 days down to three.

The agreement called for the supplier to invest some of its own money in this process. This resulted in the supplier reaping a reward based on the actual result, which turned out to be much larger than the supplier otherwise would have received. A supplier typically works on a 20 percent gross margin which, in this case, would have yielded approximately $120,000, a modest annual profit on the account.

Instead, as an incentive for the supplier to invest some of its own money, the supplier took 10 percent of the first-year savings (which netted an immodest $1 million reward). Interestingly, the buyer was also pleased because it regarded the savings as "found money" and a steal for its bottom line. It was able to achieve a $10 million saving on the $500,000 investment!

*Case Study 2: How JCPenney and CF Data saved on check collection.* Check collection has been contracted out for years. When companies get a bad check, they try to collect it once; then they send it to a collection organization (most large retailers in the U.S. use 10 to 20 of these), servicing different regions of the U.S.

For competitive reasons, JCPenney decided to take an outsourcing approach to check collection. Check collection, in terms of a commodity, is singularly the least glamorous commodity or service I can think of. This makes it an unlikely candidate for mutual cooperation between a buyer and supplier. However, in this case study, we find one of the finest examples of the value resulting from a partnership based on the idea of building business objectives into the outsourced process. JCPenney decided to move from its traditional multi-collector mode to a single-supplier outsourcing approach. After a significant amount of research, it signed a long-term contract and turned over its check collection processes to CF Data.

As in many outsourcing relationships, the underlying business assumptions changed after their deal was negotiated. In this instance, there was a shift in the economy. Credit limits had been relaxed, and more lax credit policies permeated, resulting in a decrease in the ability of the consumers to pay their debts. The percentage of checks that were collectable decreased, and this showed up as an increase in bad debt expense for JCPenney.

This phenomenon had very little to do with the supplier's performance, but JCPenney naturally blamed the supplier. Moreover, JCPenney had been riding a bull market for a long time. Also, its in-store sales were no longer improving because the company had saturated its market. Again, some of the JCPenney people blamed the supplier.

Fortunately, the executive in charge of this area—a man of vision—recognized that what the company really wanted to do was to focus on reducing bad debt, rather than deciding where to place blame. JCPenney assumed a business-oriented objective and turned to its supplier to accomplish this result.

The goal was to reduce bad debt, and the best way to accomplish that was to increase the quality of the bad debt. The way to increase quality bad debt is to improve the store policy. For instance, it is best not to take checks that are under 300 in serial number. Authorization policies and systems need to be improved and enforced. Basically, the authorization system checks both a positive and a negative file to see whether a customer is qualified or has bounced checks in the past. Obviously, a store should be reluctant to take a person's check if there is a history of not paying off the debts.

The two parties took a variety of initiatives. They split up their responsibilities, and the supplier made a significant investment in the retailer. This became one of those rare instances where the supplier actually benefited from its investment without having to share value. Why? Because the improved process took less effort, and the supplier was paid per check collected. A bounced check incurs a $10 to $25 fee to the collector, and the supplier kept a portion of that for its service. By increasing its efficiency, it made more money per inventory. The fact is, a consumer either is or is not going to pay the debt—it's that simple. The supplier's ability to spend less time working with people who would not pay their debts created revenue.

Significant investment was necessary on both sides, and the savings that resulted were also large on both sides. JCPenney invested in changing its organization's procedures, and CF Data put in a significant investment to improve training at each of the buyer's stores.

The supplier also made a commitment to adjusting its collections process so it could collect sooner. It is a fact that, as receivables age, the probability of collecting them goes down. The buyer brought its receivables collections in house, thereby compressing that cycle time, which helped lower the bad debt.

This is a classic example of how to turn a commodity supplier into an asset by focusing on a business objective. Had the buyer not given the supplier an incentive to spend the necessary $150,000 to improve the buyer's training, the arrangement would not have been successful.

Alternatively, the buyer in the beginning could have just fired its supplier because the collection ratio was going down and switched to another collection company. The risk would have been that the new company might do a worse job, and it would have taken another two years before the buyer could have determined the performance of the new supplier. Because JCPenney and CF Data had enlightened management who used this incentive technique, they achieved a real win-win situation.

*Case Study 3: The little company that roared.* When I was introduced to CTC Communications (CTC), it was a small telecommunications company going through a shift in strategy. CTC, which sold telephone services on behalf of Bell Atlantic Corporation, became threatened when Bell Atlantic shrank the commission it paid to agents. In addition, CTC believed that it could substantially increase its competitive position and company valuation by changing its business model to retain its customers through becoming a reseller of telecommunication services as well as a facilities-based outsourcing provider of these same services.

The first step in this process seemed relatively straightforward, as CTC already had most of the personnel and technology in place to accomplish the switch to a reseller; however, the second phase of the plan seemed out of reach.

CTC had no in-house expertise capable of building and then running a large carrier-quality network. The market for telecommunications engineers was very tight. That, coupled with market perception of CTC as a small company, made it unlikely that CTC could hire and retain the personnel needed to accomplish this ambitious task. The consultants and contractors specializing in this area were already fully committed with large, long-term contracts; the Bell Atlantics and AT&Ts had already sucked up all the engineering talent available.

Adding to this problem was the urgency of putting in a high-quality network, which, if accomplished in under a year, would give CTC a substantial advantage over its competitors. Furthermore, while the network was being put into place, CTC could not take time and attention away from its critical move from an agent to a reseller.

If the goals could be met, though, it would result in a probable equity valuation increase of over 10 times the then market capitalization of the company. It was make or break time!

CTC turned to outsourcing as a way to accomplish its goals, and I assisted in structuring this unique deal. CTC decided to turn over the control of this important project to an outsourcing supplier that would build and then run the network for CTC. By offering the opportunity of a long-term contract, CTC attracted the attention of several of the premier suppliers in this area of expertise.

Even so, CTC did not believe that those potential suppliers had the same sort of motivation to quickly build and run a cost-effective network for CTC, as they would have had for larger companies. In fact, it soon became apparent that, under the contract structure the suppliers offered, the suppliers would not have an incentive to deliver a network sooner than well beyond the timeframe needed, nor would they commit to provide high-quality service. It was clear that CTC was not going to get the best and the brightest of a supplier's staff because it would be one of the supplier's smaller customers. Without the economic clout of its competitors, CTC also needed assistance from the supplier to negotiate with the hardware suppliers. Once again, it was apparent that the suppliers would place their larger customers' interests before CTC's.

This is the solution CTC decided upon. Once it had established a fair price for the service through a competitive bidding process, it approached the leading supplier and offered a unique proposition. If the supplier would put at risk some of its fee to build the network, CTC would match this amount, dollar for dollar, with a reward based on performance.

The performance criteria were split into two areas. A significant portion of the fee would be withheld and paid only if the supplier demonstrated that it had built a high-quality network and that the network had met the objective of industry-standard metrics after three months of operation. This gave the supplier an incentive to build a high-quality network and run it with a very high level of quality. The second portion of the incentive was allocated to encourage the supplier to accomplish the network build-out on time—or earlier, if possible. Anyone familiar with the art of network build-out will immediately recognize the strong probability that this process usually will run well over the time allocated and cost significantly more than anticipated.

The buyer and the supplier then established a completion date, based on the supplier's proposed target date. The arrangement was agreed upon that, for every day the network was late, the supplier would pay the buyer $12,000; for every day the network was early, the buyer would pay the supplier an additional $12,000. This simple incentive structure had the remarkable effect of aligning the two companies' motivations. Both companies wanted the project to be early; both wanted to avoid, at all cost, any delays; and both companies wanted to ensure that the network was of the highest quality.

The supplier immediately put its best people on the relationship and used every ounce of its credibility with the hardware vendors to ensure that CTC got the best products at the best prices when they were needed. This resulted in savings for the buyer that far exceeded the bonus it paid. CTC was able to show its internal management that the supplier was working for CTC's best interests and could be trusted to make critical decisions without micro management. I have rarely seen such a beneficial relationship and resulting synergy. Both parties treat each other with the utmost respect while continuing to be flexible, yet driven, to common goals. These two companies avoid all the negative potentials of outsourcing and capture the vast potential it holds.

## Additional Contributions

Many of today's outsourcing suppliers, particularly data processing companies, aggressively sell their capability of making additional business contributions well beyond their ability to deliver their core services. The best practice lies in the buyer developing initiatives in projects where the supplier can take specific action (either on its own or jointly with the buyer).

If the supplier must discern where the potential for making an additional contribution lies, little of value may result. Of course, a supplier who has vast experience and expertise in handling certain kinds of processes may well be able to suggest improvements to a buyer's ideas about how to create more value in that particular area. But what is in view here is a business contribution that lies outside the area that is the focus of the primary outsourced process. If the initiative is left to the supplier, it is unlikely that it will be able to identify the key needs of the buyer.

Please note that the supplier's "bundling" of services is not to be confused with the making of a specific additional business contribution. Suppliers can, and do, make substantial contributions to business objectives; but a wise buyer will not leave this to chance. A buyer cannot assume that additional contributions of the supplier would result automatically from purchasing a bundle of services that was originally designed for other than its own situations.

If a company wants to take advantage of the potential capability of an outsourcing supplier to make a contribution that is additional to the key service that was originally focused on, the relationship must be structured to foster, identify and manage the contributions. Additional contribution from the supplier is what happened in the three case studies just described. How to determine what to pay for the contribution will be explained in Chapter 7, as well as how to handle the associated risks.

By following these simple principles, more value will be created in an outsourcing relationship; the result will be a total performance vehicle of unparalleled power. The energy and investment, in terms of managing an outsourcing relationship, can yield huge dividends. Remember that it takes teamwork to haul in tons of gold.

# Chapter 6

# MAKE SURE
# IT'S GOLD

*"One accurate measurement is worth
a thousand expert opinions."*
—Rear Admiral Grace Murray Hopper,
U.S. Navy

Those early alchemists dabbled with elements and made many discoveries during the process. Bacon, for instance, discovered gunpowder; and Geber, who lived in the 700s, discovered mercury, nitric acid and nitrate of silver. But they didn't have the necessary measurements for elements to make gold; consequently, all but a few died as paupers.

In a contracting situation, the buyer gives instructions and then develops inspections to ensure its instructions have been carried out. In outsourcing, the buyer and supplier establish service levels to measure the results the buyer requires. Then they continually monitor the metrics to make sure the buyer is receiving the results the buyer is paying for.

The temptation for a buyer to try to fix problems instead of working through its supplier can be overwhelming. Many a buyer has started down this path only to find out that their attempts were fruitless or further compounded the situation. This is because, in turning over the ownership of the process to the supplier, the buyer also has turned over the ability to dictate remedies. As these factors emerge in the outsourcing relationship, the potential for conflict increases significantly.

In high-stakes encounters, the supplier has a significant contractual advantage (because of its points of leverage, together with its monopoly power as the sole source for any answers). As you can see, it would not be a fair fight, and the natural "slope of the hill" would be in the supplier's favor. When the slope of the hill is against the buyer, it is time to change the venue for the event to a more even playing field—or the buyer will inevitably lose the game or battle. The way buyers accomplish this is through the following mechanisms.

### How to Establish Service Levels

We set service levels in three steps. The first step is for buyers to define what they are buying by establishing a scope and definition of the services. This scope must have clear boundaries that enable both supplier and buyer to determine what is in and out of scope. It is important that this scope be defined at the process level but not be overly prescriptive of how the process is to be delivered. Defining the scope of services to be purchased is the first step in establishing fair and objective metrics because metrics or service levels tend to cluster around process boundaries. At some point, the supplier must come into contact with the rest of the buyer's company or with other vendors; this contact can cause friction and bring opportunity for mischief. Another reason to clarify the scope in the beginning is that this is the only point when the results of the process can be measured objectively. Without establishing a clear scope and a crisp, definite boundary, the effort to objectively measure the results is doomed to failure.

The second step is to establish clear, objective and reliable measures or "metrics" of the required results. By relying on those metrics, the buyer can allow the supplier the freedom to own the process. The third step is to establish the most important metric—a fair price for the services. (I will cover how to establish pricing in Chapter 7.)

**Establishing Metrics**

Without a yardstick, there is neither measurement nor control, notes management consultant Pravin M. Shah. I am always bemused with outsourcing executives who comfortably assert their customers should trust them and that service levels or metrics are unnecessary.

Nothing could be further from the truth. Outsourcing without adequate measurements always ends in tears—initially for the buyer and, eventually, also for the supplier. To manage an outsourcing relationship without establishing adequate service levels is like driving a car without a steering wheel—it will invariably end in disaster. The bigger and faster the car, the bigger the potential disaster!

I often see suppliers give great lip service to the need for metrics but then try to thwart meaningful implementations at every turn. Even when there are no consequences for non-performance, they are reluctant to agree to metrics.

As a former supplier, I believe that this strong aversion to metrics is simply an attempt to avoid accountability. It is true that many of the metrics proposed by buyers tend to measure the "how," rather than the "what," and so tend to encourage suppliers to adopt counterproductive behavior. Nonetheless, I believe that outsourcing relationships without metrics are doomed to end in conflict. Fair metrics, which focus on the results of the process, are an absolute necessity for the industry, as well as for the individual buyers and suppliers that comprise the industry.

Historically, we have tried to manage outsourcing relationships through contracts. Certainly the need for solid contracts is indisputable, for they create the basis for risk allocation and define the terms under which the parties agree to work together. However, when either party attempts to manage the relationship through contractual provisions, it can quickly end up in an adversarial position. Both parties can become slaves to the letter of the law and start looking for ways around contractual constraints. This creates an unhealthy relationship.

What is the alternative? It is to manage by service levels. If the buyer has adequately defined the results it seeks from outsourcing, it measures those results, allowing the outsourcer the freedom to reengineer the process and eliminate unnecessary and non-value-added steps as long as the buyer continues to get what it is paying for. For example, companies like BP Amoco do not care where their accounting functions are housed as long as they are assured that their suppliers are providing high-quality service consistent with contract obligations.

### The Necessity

In outsourcing, you get what you inspect—not what you expect. Trust (or the lack of it) has nothing to do with the need for service levels or metrics. No organization, whether internal or external, can be allowed to operate without ongoing guidance and performance reviews.

Outsourcing is the transfer from buyer to supplier of responsibility for a process. Since the supplier needs to be able to control the process, it is through agreement about the levels of service that the buyer retains the influence that it must retain if it is to ensure its satisfaction. This is, in fact, the only effective source of control available to the buyer.

Service levels and pricing are the major sources of communications between buyers and suppliers. Measurements give the supplier a way to ensure it is producing the agreed-upon results and a way to make adjustments, if need be.

A relationship without service levels allows the supplier to determine the direction of the relationship. This is undesirable for three reasons.

First, suppliers have their own profit and revenue imperatives. This, of course, is healthy, but the buyer is purchasing a service and needs to ensure the results will be fair. When inadequate metrics exist, the temptation for the supplier is to attempt to achieve increased profitability by reducing the quality of the service. When a buyer establishes adequate metrics and backs them up with appropriate consequences, the supplier must focus on process improvement to achieve profitability. This results in an improved process from which both parties benefit.

Second, the buyer can set only the business direction for the outsourced service. The supplier is part of an integrated supply chain; it would be rare and extremely surprising if a supplier that is allowed to set parameters would bring alignment with a buyer's objectives.

Third, without adequate service levels with which to measure the required results, the supplier's need for profit growth may force it to try to move components of the process outside the scope of the services so that it can then charge extra for them and satisfy the profit needs of the supplier. With an adequate scope definition as well as objective metrics, the supplier will be free to reengineer the process to accomplish its profit goals.

In contracting, it is easy to measure whether the supplier has performed the task as specified. But how can one objectively measure an intangible process? It is not enough just to feel good about a process. For example, how clean was your last hotel room when you walked into it? How do you measure how clean a room is? Can you define what constitutes a clean room and how to measure these attributes? I was challenged on this issue by a potential client and was forced to adopt the old Supreme Court definition of pornography—"I know it when I see it." This may work for our Supreme Court, but it will end in dismal failure for an outsourcing relationship.

Usually, we need to measure multiple attributes of a desired result. For example, in the desktop arena, we may want good service from the help desk. One attribute may be how fast the phone is answered when someone calls; another may be how long the caller is put on hold, or the frequency of putting callers on hold. Another requirement may be the quality of advice given, and how many tiers the caller must go through in order to resolve a specific problem.

Now, imagine that one measures only some, not all, of these qualities. Maybe an enterprising supplier will agree to pick up the phone within an acceptable time and then put the caller on hold for three or four minutes. Or this supplier might cut costs by having an unqualified person speak with the caller initially, then forward the call to a series of people before the caller gets to speak with the true experts. Without service levels in place to measure what is really important about a process, how can the buyer know if the supplier is providing value or whether an alternative supplier would be preferable?

## What Buyers Should Measure

A common trap when establishing service levels is to measure the wrong things. In the help desk example, I have seen service levels established for the number of people who must be present at the help desk, or established for the qualifications and training they receive. At first blush, such metrics look innocent enough and seem to be a good idea for a buyer seeking to avoid the types of problems noted above. However, as we dig a little deeper, we can see that these metrics are prescriptive and remove accountability for the result away from the supplier.

In this help desk instance, the supplier only has to comply with the metrics to satisfy its contractual commitments. It does not matter that the quality of the results is not what the customer wants; it only matters that the right number of people with the right amount of training are available and on call at a certain point of time. In such an instance, the supplier's energy will go into meeting those requirements and not into providing outstanding help desk services.

It is a double injustice that the supplier cannot invest in new technologies or redesign the process to allow it to make more money because the metrics will not allow the supplier to benefit from such investments. The result is worse service and a poorer supplier. Not surprisingly, many suppliers resist implementing service levels and, when pushed, agree only to a bare minimum. From their point of view, the fewer service levels used, the more opportunity they have to structure the process in their favor. There is no problem in allowing them to structure the process; however, a wise buyer will ensure that there are sufficient metrics to guarantee the results it is buying.

Measuring the impact of the contribution on the business objectives is the next step. In the outsourcing of facilities management of a building, for example, service levels would need to be developed to measure the temperature in each office; how manicured the lawns are; how clean the bathrooms and floors are; and whether or not there is an adequate level of security in the building. These are the results that a buyer would purchase. To try to prescribe the number of staff, the way in which power will be procured, or the type of lawn equipment to be used will have a detrimental effect on both the level of service and the profits for the supplier.

These metrics may prove to be restrictive to the supplier and not be helpful to the buyer. A better solution would be to have a customer satisfaction metric to gauge the overall satisfaction of the people using the facilities—combined with a metric that measures worker productivity, the ease of expanding and contracting the facility to meet changing patterns of growth, and the total cost of provisioning work space.

These measurements align suppliers much closer with the business objectives of the buyer. When suppliers have meaningful positive and negative consequences based on worker productivity, they can be expected to rethink the ergonomics of the office space. A supplier that is measured against the total cost to provide work space may invest in innovative supply chain management strategies to reduce the cleaning and security costs. It will work to reduce the tax basis to further reduce overall cost.

Another example is benefits administration. We assisted Haliburton Company with outsourcing its benefits administration to Hewitt Associates. Haliburton wanted to measure the normal service levels, including the promptness of Hewitt's actions and the accuracy of the information it provided in its administrative reports. In addition, Halliburton decided to measure the number of benefit cases that went to arbitration. Halliburton had established an arbitration vehicle some years earlier to ensure that every employee was treated fairly. This helped to avoid costly legal fees.

Halliburton knew the average number of arbitration cases that were generated per thousand employees over a 12-month period. It reasoned if Hewitt were to align its interests with Halliburton, it must be held accountable for keeping the number of incidents to a minimum. In this way Halliburton was able to establish a metric on an issue it really cared about and that was aligned with its corporate goals.

Clearly, in payroll outsourcing, it is important that employees receive their checks on time. It is also important that tax deductions be accurate, that tax money be deposited on time with the IRS, that payroll be reported on time and accurately. The parties should not try to measure the quality of the supplier's staff nor the employee turnover in key positions. Only the results of the process should be measured.

When logistics are outsourced, key results (such as inventory turns and out-of-stock occurrences) should be measured. Metrics for staffing levels, compliance with OS9000 standards, and other such metrics should be avoided. By all means, do not measure the education level of the supplier's warehouse guard or dictate the processes used to develop the software.

### Challenges of Measuring

One of the key elements and central truths of outsourcing is that a service that is difficult to measure will be difficult to manage. This should give every buyer pause as they attempt to develop metrics.

Application support is an excellent example of this truth (as anyone who has outsourced this function can attest). It is difficult to measure exactly what is being delivered in application support. Historically, buyers have resorted to a time-and-materials pricing vehicle, with no measurements available regarding quality, cycle time, appropriateness of costs or resource use. Some buyers have had some success with utilizing function point service levels; however, the esoteric nature of these metrics still makes the service levels difficult to design, implement and administer.

Many outsourced services are difficult to manage because buyers do not outsource the entire process. The reasons for this are numerous and often center around middle management's desire to control the process. Too often these managers do not understand the nature of outsourcing or trust it to work when they do not totally control the process. Whenever you fracture or divide the process, it becomes very difficult to establish metrics around the desired results. The only way a buyer can get what it wants is to give the supplier total control; the supplier cannot have an impact on the outsourced process when it is not in control of some of the factors that influence the outcome. The result is an outsourcing relationship that is difficult to manage and that usually does not live up to its full potential to create value.

There has been rapid growth of outsourcing in non-IT areas, such as building maintenance, vehicle maintenance and logistics. This is partly due to the existence of easy-to-understand service levels in these processes. If measurement is intuitive and easy, it allows for the rapid growth of outsourcing. For example, in utility outsourcing, it is easy to understand whether a meter has been read correctly and whether an invoice has been sent to a customer.

The following diagram depicts two continuums to aid in the understanding of metrics.

# Metric Framework

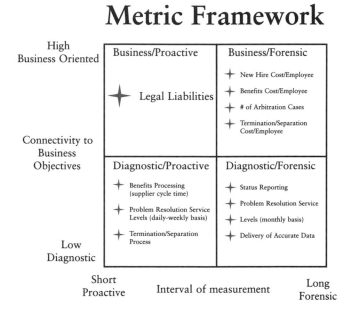

The vertical axis is the degree of connectivity to a buyer's business objectives. Metrics at the lower end of this scale are called *diagnostic*. They are measures of the results from the outsourced service (not a measure on how effective those results have been in creating value for the buyer). In this diagram, the horizontal axis represents how frequently the buyer interrogates the metric. Metrics on the left side of this continuum are called *forensic.*

### Effects of Diagnostic and Business-Oriented Metrics

Diagnostic metrics measure the results of an outsourced service. Good examples of this from the world of IT would be the availability of a telecommunications computer network or, in plain English, the percentage of the time the network is available and not experiencing an interruption in service. Another example is network response-time, that is, the time it takes for a transaction to traverse the network successfully.

Network availability or response-time measurement is a meaningful way to assess the performance of a network. These are examples of diagnostic service levels; they diagnose the performance of the service, but they are not directly linked to business performance. Of course, they ultimately impact business performance. Historically, nearly all outsourcing service levels have been exclusively diagnostic. This makes a lot of sense, as the primary results are what is measured, and the results are what the buyer purchases.

At the other end of the horizontal scale are business-oriented metrics. These metrics measure the impact on a buyer's business objectives. One example of this is the Halliburton/Hewitt relationship. The outsourced process was benefits administration, and the supplier was the interface with all the health insurance companies. A business objective for

Halliburton was to cut or, at least, to better control the cost of its insurance. Another of its business objectives was to reduce the number of arbitration cases (those cases were associated with benefits which, at the time, were the source of many of their arbitration disputes). As in most business objectives, the supplier did not have complete control over the results.

After many heated debates, the parties agreed to measure these results and tie incentives for the supplier to successful reductions in arbitration cases and lower per-employee benefits costs. The penalties or negative consequences were reserved for the diagnostic metrics (including fast response time to employee questions, accurate answers about benefits policies), over which the supplier had complete control. By allowing the supplier to make a little more money in this way, the buyer also made more money through lower legal and benefits costs. This generous approach on the part of the buyer proved to be both effective and efficient and resulted in increased value for both parties.

When implementing business-oriented metrics, a supplier must speak in the language of the buyer's business. The buyer, on the other hand, must not overplay this tool and must ensure that it only uses these metrics to align the supplier to what is really important to the business. If these metrics are implemented without due thought, the buyer could easily overpay for services without gaining any real increase in value.

A good indicator of whether you are dealing with a business-oriented service level or a diagnostic-oriented service level is the language used to state it. A business-oriented service level cannot be stated in technical terms; it must be stated in business terms. The on-time arrival of a truck in a logistics business, for example, can impact out-of-order stocking of a warehouse; however, that term would be associated with the service, not with the business. In the Halliburton/Hewitt example, the diagnostic metrics were the mean time to answer a phone call. The business metrics related to the cost of providing the benefits and the number of arbitration cases. The business metrics came directly from the lexicon of the company's senior executives.

### Effects of Proactive and Forensic Metrics

The term "forensic" is a colorful one, often used in the context of a post mortem, and it is just such an image that I wish to evoke here. If there is a lengthy time lag between interrogating metrics (how often the metric is inspected), a poor result will have already significantly impacted the business. At that point, a buyer's only real options are to penalize the supplier—or, as we say in Texas, "Get a rope, there's going to be a hanging."

Relying primarily on forensic metrics is like driving a car forward while looking through the rear-view mirror. Information you gain from your rear-view mirror is helpful, but it won't prevent you from hitting something. Be sure that you also provide for, and pay attention to, proactive metrics that look forward to where you are headed.

On the left side of the interval of measurement continuum are proactive metrics. When a metric or service level is interrogated (inspected) on a frequent basis, it is called a proactive metric. Now, clearly, it is not truly proactive because a failure or poor result cannot be predicted; it is proactive in the sense that action can be taken before significant business damage is done. Proactive metrics must be inspected often enough so the supplier can change behavior before it has a major consequence for the buyer's business.

These types of metrics allow buyer and supplier to cooperate quickly to minimize any damage and to take hasty action to rectify the situation. Although they can be expensive to implement and nearly always require automated capture, monitoring devices build good will on both sides of the fence and foster cooperation instead of blame.

An example of a proactive metric is when a buyer monitors a call center's average time to respond to an incoming call on an hourly basis. An increase in the time it takes to answer the phone may be indicative of a staffing shortage, which can be rectified by the supplier if it is caught quickly. Alternatively, it could indicate that the customers are experiencing a major problem with the product or some other variable out of the supplier's control and in the sphere of influence of the buyer. In this case the buyer will want to examine its options to see what actions it can take to remedy the situation.

The transparency and immediacy of proactive metrics concentrates a supplier's mind and increases its motivation to rectify the problem. In instances where there are no proactive metrics, the supplier may work feverishly to try to fix a problem, but the customer will not know how to help. Returning to our call center example, the buyer may be in a position to work on the deeper issue of why the volume of calls has increased unexpectedly, while at the same time the supplier works to increase the staffing of the call center.

To build an effective relationship, constant and effective communication must be built in. The purpose of proactive service levels is not to punish or reward but, rather, to generate appropriate, corrective action when necessary. For example, I may be outsourcing a help desk or call center. If I recognize that the amount of time my customers spend on hold when they call in has gone from a 30-second average to a three, four or 10-minute average, the supplier can immediately take action before it impacts the general satisfaction of my customers. It may negatively affect a couple of my customers, but I will not have lost many of them.

A word of caution is necessary when considering implementing proactive metrics. Do not confuse event alerts with service levels. Service levels are, by definition, statistical averages over some period of time. To focus on specific events is to interfere with the process. Tracking the performance over time, rather than looking at specific events, is what should be done. This is a subtle, but important distinction. Once again, the buyer is not to take on responsibility for the process; instead, it should focus on results and encourage cooperation.

Different processes will have different natural interrogation periods. A proactive metric of inventory turns could be interrogated on a monthly basis; a forensic metric might be done on a yearly basis. A proactive metric of network availability may be to interrogate by the hour or by the minute; a forensic metric would be to measure by the month. The type of process drives the interrogation period and whether it is proactive or forensic.

A word to my supplier friends: unlike a good wine, bad news does not get better with age. A buyer who has been alerted about a problem early on is more willing to work in partnership with the supplier to solve the problem. If the supplier waits until the end of a month or an entire quarter to alert the buyer to a problem, the time lag allows frustration to build up. By then the buyer will want to punish the supplier more than cooperate in correcting the situation. (Here comes that rope again!)

How many diagnostic service levels are needed depends on the kind of process being outsourced. Since service levels are the primary means of buyer control, the buyer will want to ensure that its interests are adequately covered and the expected results are measured sufficiently in order to avoid future problems. Typically, there are a significant number of expected results, all of them needing service levels or metrics. As explained earlier, incompletely measuring the results can spawn unfortunate supplier behavior, with little or no possibility for correction. In the end, there is no right number; however, smart buyers always seem to want more than the suppliers want to provide.

Another challenge is that it is possible to over measure. The trick is to measure sufficient attributes—but not too many. If the buyer measures attributes it does not care about, and applies consequences to results, it will unnecessarily raise the cost of the service being bought and squander the supplier's energy and investment. This would make the transaction unattractive for both sides.

The right number of business-oriented service levels is easier to predict. Business metrics should be used sparingly, as too many will confuse both the supplier and the buyer. These metrics are like a rudder guiding a ship—they keep the relationship stable and allow the parties to keep moving forward, no matter how bad the weather. If too many rudders are in place at one time, however, the ship will receive conflicting signals and flounder. I recommend that no more than one or two of these metrics be employed at a time for any given process.

**The Dangers and Problems in Metrics**

Several difficulties and dangers often tend to occur when metrics are developed and implemented.

Suppose a buyer outsources a process such as desktop processing. To supply the service, the supplier hires the very same people who had been doing that work for the buyer. The buyer then expects to receive better service the next day. Well, why would that be? Nothing has changed; the same people are working with the same equipment, and the same process is being used. It is just too early to expect to see any improvement. The supplier will need to train the former staff, bring in a new process and invest in new equipment. The supplier must constantly reengineer the process in order to meet its profit goals. Buyers need to be patient with their suppliers as they first take over a process.

Like an old-fashioned safety razor blade, service levels cut both ways. The use of service levels brings accountability to both the supplier and buyer sides. It is unreasonable to expect a supplier to perform well when it has not been given the appropriate information, cooperation or resources to complete its task. Often, the buyer will need to introduce the disciplines of service levels on its own process—particularly those that interface with the outsourced area. In these instances, the buyer becomes, in effect, accountable to the supplier to ensure that it is a part of the value chain it controls.

An example of this can be seen in some desktop outsourcing relationships where the buyer has decided to manage the purchasing of new equipment. If the equipment is not provided according to the agreed schedules, the supplier cannot be held accountable for timely installation at the user's desk.

The objectivity of metrics forces a buyer to shoulder accountability for its business. As long as the results are delivered in conformance with the prescribed metrics, the buyer has no cause for complaint. If the buyer wishes to change the results or becomes dissatisfied with the level of performance prescribed in the service levels, it must develop new metrics and negotiate their acceptance. Through this act, the buyer is changing the services that it is buying and might be asked to pay an additional fee. This is the nature of an arms-length relationship. If they are unwilling to live with the new terms as negotiated, it is time to find a new supplier or live with the outcome.

One problem with measuring results is the possibility that a supplier might at some time fail to provide the expected results. This raises the ugly specter of revenge. On a more constructive note, if a buyer has not received what it is paying for, it should not have to pay, or at least not pay as much. In all outsourcing relationships, careful consideration should be given to establish just and sure consequences for a supplier's poor performance.

Meaningful consequences act in much the same way as live ammunition—they serve to concentrate the mind of the supplier. However, there is a place and a time for consequences. They should not be applied to proactive metrics because these are used to galvanize action; instead, they should be reserved for forensic metrics.

It is not always necessary to assign a consequence to every forensic service level. The parties can arrange for a percentage of the monthly service price to be put at risk and have the buyer be able to distribute these over specified service levels. For example, a customer may choose to reserve 10 percent of a supplier's revenue to hold at risk should the supplier fail to provide the services as defined in the service levels they negotiated in the contract. The buyer can then further refine this model by allocating a higher percentage of the reserved amount to important metrics. After giving 30 or 60 days' notice, the buyer can then reallocate a percentage of the consequences onto different service levels.

The net effect is that, if there is a portfolio of service levels, it is quite appropriate to measure things that may not have a consequence or penalty assigned. They may be less important attributes, yet they are vehicles to help in determining if things are out of balance. If these results turn out to be more significant than expected, the buyer can choose to reallocate the supplier's risk to ensure close scrutiny. On the other hand, the buyer is restricted from adding more risk to the relationship, as it cannot change the overall percentage at stake. This arrangement requires that the buyer make a choice; the choice then becomes a signal to the supplier as to what is really important.

For business metrics, where the supplier does not control all of the variables that impact the results, incentives are often more helpful than penalties. When business objectives are met, additional value is created. This creates the opportunity for rewards, as opposed to penalties, from the buyer to the supplier. One can build incentives based on actual value creation. These types of service levels or metrics can be used to repair dysfunctional outsourcing relationships and realign a supplier's interest and motivation with the buyer's business. In effect, they act as the pressure-release valve in the container.

**Automating the Metrics**

Good diagnostic service levels should be a by-product of the process result. In most cases, it is possible to find automated vehicles to monitor these metrics. A classic mistake is to rely on subjective criteria, such as a survey or a manual process (which are subject to human error and motivations). These types of metrics do not invite accuracy, often are not objective; and they court disagreement. The raw data should speak for itself.

The best service levels come from use of automated processes that give access to raw data, not data that has been massaged. For example, in the case of benefits administration, the time it takes to pick up an incoming employee's question can be monitored automatically by the phone switch, and the call-back rate can be automatically calculated from the call center software. In this instance, no human effort is required, and the results are not open to question.

Administering service levels does not add value to a process. I strongly encourage all suppliers to automate as many service levels as possible. A buyer does not need an army of people inspecting results, but it needs to be alerted when a service level target is not met. Through automation of this process, the buyer can focus on the important issues while leaving the supplier to run the process.

## Continual Improvement

There has been a movement to try to build into outsourcing contracts the imperative for continual improvement. An example would be to require a five percent improvement in service every year and a five percent drop in price. In practice, though, this concept has significant limitations.

First, if there is room to reduce price (other than the first drop in cost after the supplier has finished its reengineering or capital expenditure), then that price should be agreed to up-front. A buyer who relies on the supplier's learning curve to lower cost also needs to rely on a shorter-term contract. It would be best for the supplier to discount the price for the learning curve by a certain degree because of the risk associated with it. Buyers often unwittingly create great problems for suppliers and themselves. It would be more equitable to nurture a long-term relationship by using a short-term contract.

It is, of course, possible to include provisions in a contract to require the supplier to meet industry benchmark standards. It is even possible for these service levels to be set so that they become progressively higher as time passes.

But it may be unwise to expect a supplier to reduce its costs during the life of a contract. Suppliers often can defeat such clauses because they can demonstrate some customization that was requested by the buyer but that was not anticipated in the original transaction and so claim that the agreed-upon changes are no longer relevant. In fact, a clever supplier often gets the buyer to agree to delete such clauses before it makes any buyer-requested changes. This again emphasizes the desirability to have shorter-term contracts and longer-term relationships. When a contract is about to expire, the supplier often will be more obliging regarding price.

In my experience, benchmarking and other measuring vehicles are substitutes often put in place by the buyer to try to fix the problems inherent in an overly long contract period. Historically, these substitutes do not work out well for the buyers.

## Chapter 7

# THE PRICE OF GOLD

*Quality in a product or service is not what the
supplier puts in. It is what the customer gets out
and is willing to pay for.*
—Peter Drucker, business consultant and professor

Before the aspiring alchemists subjected themselves to the rigors and hard work of an alchemy
apprenticeship, they must have convinced themselves
that the end result would be worth all their effort
and risk. Similarly, today's potential outsourcing
participants must be sure that the effort and risk of
undertaking outsourcing will pay off, just as the
company that is extracting gold from the cast-off ore
at Cripple Creek must ensure that it can sell its gold
for more than it cost to extract it.

Today's outsourcing buyers must be clear that
they are getting a better economic deal by outsourcing than by keeping the process in-house. They do

this by comparing the total price they expect to pay in an outsourcing relationship with the total cost of providing the same services themselves. But to accomplish this, they must establish a fair and objective pricing mechanism. It is this mechanism which we will examine in this chapter.

## Pricing Is More than Establishing a Cost

Beyond establishing a cost, pricing can serve at least two other purposes.

*A Means of Communication.* The pricing structure can be more important than the price itself. It becomes a primary means of communication between suppliers and buyers; in fact, it is the most important and most enduring form of communication between them. The reason it endures is that when people shift (as they often do in these relationships), what is left behind is the pricing and service levels. Service levels often can be ignored, but pricing is always apparent. In our cost-driven world, it is what people's eyes go to first of all; price is a signal.

Along with service levels and management meetings or correspondence, understanding is driven through pricing. I am sure most of my readers can readily agree that nothing gets attention like missing a budget. I cannot overemphasize the importance of pricing. In a results-based deal, it is best to structure price (if possible) around the results; it also becomes the way the relationship is managed and how the participants communicate. In a fractured process where results cannot adequately be defined, pricing should be structured around cost drivers.

For example, one buyer chose to structure pricing for its outsourced medical underwriting process by paying for the information that it received on each of its insurance applicants. Because selling insurance is a highly competitive field, the time it takes to approve an application is important. This makes the elapsed time between application and approval an important metric.

The buyer chose to tie the price it paid to the time it took the supplier to provide the information. Applications that were processed in less than five days carried a premium, while applications processed over 10 days carried a penalty. In this way, the supplier was financially rewarded when it created value for the insurance company and shared the risk when the information was less valuable to the insurance company.

This pricing vehicle worked because the insurance company outsourced an entire process. If it had chosen to outsource a fractured process—only the lab testing, for example—this innovative option would not have been available. Since the supplier could not control enough of the process, this structure would have been unfair.

*A charge-back vehicle.* Pricing is also a form of communication to the rest of the user organization. In the event that multiple stakeholders consume services and products, it is a form of communication to those other divisions. A key and often-misunderstood benefit of outsourcing is its potential to be an effective charge-back vehicle; it allows the buyer to drive accountability within its own departments or subsidiaries.

In outsourced IT, for example, if pricing is done by desktop, then each of the consuming divisions knows how many desktops it is using and can see the cost per desktop. That is good pricing. They understand that if they add more desktops, the price will go up; if they reduce the number of desktops, the price will go down. That is a very effective form of communication.

Over the years, I have seen the lack of an effective charge-back mechanism contribute to buyer dissatisfaction. The problem arises when a process is outsourced and the bills come in to one central administrative point. If they are paid out of a corporate administration account and not allocated back to the users in the buyer's departments, those departmental users, in effect, receive a free resource with no accountability for its use. The buyer has thus broken the law of cause and effect.

Undisciplined use of a free resource encourages the using departments to make demands with no or little concern for the cost; after all, they are not going to pay for it and, at worst, the cost will be shared by all departments through a G&A allocation. The stakeholder paying the bills (often the Chief Financial Officer) soon would find costs running out of control.

The supplier, who initially would be pleased with the additional business, would be caught in the middle. Obviously, this is not a recipe for an effective long-term relationship. In order to counter this destructive force, the buyer must implement an effective charge-back vehicle.

Having made this decision, the next problem a buyer faces is when the using departments do not understand the technical terms that the supplier uses. For example, I know few business people who really understand what a MIP is (million instructions per second) or what GIG (prefix for billion, as in gigabyte) means. Nevertheless, these are the price units that most mainframe suppliers use to charge their customers.

Typically, in an outsourcing situation, the buyer has taken a technical process and specialized knowledge and transferred it to the supplier. If the supplier bills in terms of that business unit or process, there is no one who understands the bill. If, however, the bill is for "payroll invoices," for example, then everyone intuitively understands what the bill is about.

If useful communication is to take place with user departments, the buyer's contract administration team needs to translate esoteric terms into business language. Please note that the buyer must make this translation. Most suppliers will not have the background to do this. The buyer's contract administration group will probably still want to see the cost in an industry standard structure so that it can conduct benchmarking on a periodic basis and understand whether or not it is still receiving a fair price for the services.

The need for clarity and unambiguous terms is extremely important in communication. The pricing structure either aligns the two parties' interests, or it acts to drive friction into the relationship. Where the pricing structure is obscure or hard to relate to, it drives friction into the relationship.

## Two Common Practices to Avoid

I advise buyers to avoid two pricing practices:

*1. Open-book ("cost-plus") pricing.* I have never found a cost-plus contract that worked well. Buyers often say, in effect, "I want to know what all your costs are." The inference or implication is they want to control the profit margin the supplier has. The problem with open book pricing is that it seldom works. If you think about it, cost-plus is anti-outsourcing in that it does not acknowledge that the supplier owns the process. It implies that the buyer owns the process and that the supplier is not entitled to the profits it generates; so profits are capped.

There is constant pressure on the supplier (especially if it is a public company) to increase profits and produce revenues. Cost-plus, in effect, denies suppliers their rightful ability to make money. It controls and removes the supplier's incentive to be innovative in terms of increasing the effectiveness of the process, because all gains would go to the buyer.

A further indignity is that it is almost always prescriptive. The buyer dictates how the process is to be managed through controlling the cost structure. Increases in the supplier's profits (if those profits do not come at the expense of poorer services) are rightfully the property of the supplier. A profitable supplier is in a position to assure a continued source of good services. The open book, or cost-plus practice robs outsourcing of one of its major leverage points and historically has been unproductive.

Perhaps the most unfortunate thing about cost plus is what it does to both the supplier and the buyer. Most companies are reticent to open their books to others. There is almost always friction over what is cost and who should pay for it. The open book practice nearly always creates a lot of mischief associated with disguising what costs are and what overhead is. It basically causes both parties to cheat.

*2. Bundling of unrelated costs.* The bundling of unrelated cost drivers is always an unfair pricing mechanism. Over any long-term relationship, one of the two parties will lose. For example, a supplier may combine the cost of servicing the desktop environment with the application and development process (ADM). The cost drivers dealing with the number of desktops and the velocity of technological change have little to do with the cost drivers in ADM. These include the number of application software packages the supplier must maintain and the velocity of new requirements that the users request.

Typically, bundling takes different cost drivers and different results and then prices them all together. This is usually a bad idea because it reduces the transparency of the relationship, making it more difficult for both parties to understand what is being bought and sold. An unclear understanding of what the transactions are based on interferes with communication and plays to a potentially manipulative environment.

With bundling, it is unclear if the supplier takes things out of scope, which causes the cost to go down. The supplier can't tell if the buyer is pushing things into scope. So it is a bad idea from both perspectives.

The problems occur in two areas. First, bundled pricing obscures the ability of the buyer to understand what it is buying. This will add considerable confusion into the relationship, and this confusion tends to increase. As the relationship ages, a natural adjustment needs to be made to compensate for changes in technology and business direction.

Secondly, a bundled pricing structure almost always favors the supplier. Since the supplier owns the process and has the process expertise, it is in a strong position to manipulate any discussion of changes to the relationship in its favor. Many suppliers have learned to exploit this power to increase significantly their overall economic position; some of this latent manipulative power is taken away from them when pricing is unbundled.

With unbundled pricing, it is possible to benchmark and understand the true relationship between changes in technologies and the need for price adjustments. Buyers are always better off if they can structure pricing by major cost drivers; these provide a much better understanding of what is being purchased and will communicate to both parties much more clearly.

Only with a complete process and adequately defined results can bundling pricing by results can be a good idea. In such an instance, it would provide clarity and communication.

A good example is the insurance company that outsourced its medical underwriting process. The company was able to combine the sub-process of the paramedics, who gathered the blood and urine samples, with the lab, which tested the samples. Combining these functions enabled the supplier to do two things: focus on the desired business result of providing timely information and resolve the problematic transition between the paramedics and the lab which had, up until then, been plaguing the industry.

**What Is a Fair Price?**

Price is not a function of cost; price is a function of competition. In an arms-length transaction such as outsourcing, the market typically sets the price. By "market," I do not mean an industry standard price that can be quoted. In outsourcing, given the wide variation of service levels that buyers ask for, often there is no standard price.

"Market" in outsourcing is defined as "competition." If there is no competition for a contract, then the market resembles a monopoly—and the buyer is in an unfavorable position. If "market" is defined as competition, the supplier will adjust its rate to the market. If there is no competition, the buyer will pay a negotiated rate which, in all likelihood, will be significantly above what it could receive in a competitive market. In an open bidding situation, a market price is easily established. It is the price set in the context of competition that I refer to as "market pricing."

The cost structure of the supplier is, of course, important in pricing. The mistake that buyers tend to make is not recognizing that suppliers have a right to make a profit and that their profit is not related to their cost (it is related to the market for that service). For example, in the instance of ADP and payroll processing, the issue is not what it costs ADP to produce a check; rather, it is what the market says is a fair price for processing that check.

During the negotiations, the supplier may claim it cannot meet a price without losing money. This is usually a negotiating ploy to justify its pricing. In reality, if the supplier is losing money in a competitive bidding situation, it is a high-cost provider that must differentiate itself in some other way. If the buyer is not convinced of the value of the supplier's differentiation, it would be well served to go elsewhere.

**Factors to Consider In Establishing Pricing**

One of the issues that buyers need to realize is that price is adjusted basically for risk. Risk is a factor of contractual commitments, liability limits, the amount of investment the supplier is putting into the process, and the penalties or consequences if the supplier fails to perform. If a buyer asks for an extraordinarily high level of service, it will affect how much investment the supplier must spend to accomplish the process delivery.

As an example, let's use an instance of desktop outsourcing. Say the buyer asks that all its desktops be serviced and working at a level of 99.9 percent of the time. This extraordinary level of performance requires the supplier to maintain a very high-cost infrastructure in order to accomplish that high level of availability. The supplier will need to have redundant processing so that, if one computer system goes down, another picks up the slack. The difference in the desktop world between a customary level of availability for service (say 98 or 99 percent, as opposed to 99.9 percent) is a huge difference in cost.

A naive buyer sets its service levels extremely high and doesn't understand that it can pay a significant premium because of that. Typically, as a buyer moves at the end of the spectrum to extraordinary levels of performance, the buyer increases the cost to the supplier tremendously, and that cost will be passed on to the buyer. The buyer sometimes doesn't recognize that it is doing that.

The supplier's significant investments to get the business are often traps in pricing considerations. During my stint as a supplier, we consistently overstated the amount of investments, and this practice still goes on today. It should still be possible to determine exactly what that investment is and then use this as a basis to negotiate an appropriate termination for convenience clause.

A termination for convenience clause allows the buyer to end the outsourcing contract before its contract expiration date. It is sound business practice to ensure that every outsourcing contract clearly states the cost to exit prematurely. The world is an uncertain place, and it may be necessary to terminate the contract.

However, it is also fair to compensate the supplier for the investment it made in establishing the outsourcing relationship. Typically, the up-front investment can be amortized over the life of the contract, allowing the buyer to exit with less expense after the supplier has recouped its investment.

The incremental costs to the investment over the life of the contract must be amortized. The supplier may argue that this factor must be reflected in increased cost. In my experience, some increase is justified, but not a great deal, so look at the numbers and see what they really justify. Spreading this cost over a long time does not make sense.

Furthermore, it is not wise to amortize costs over a long period in a service where the technology rapidly changes. Malcolm Forbes pointed out that five-year-old projections evidence the fact that businessmen don't always deal in facts. In such cases, the supplier must be able to replace the technology within a short time period in order to stay competitive. By establishing a long amortization schedule, the buyer, in effect, makes it unprofitable for the supplier to stay current with technology. This action reduces the quality of the service the supplier can provide.

In the event that a supplier makes an investment that spreads across multiple services, one can legitimately pull out the investment into a separate vehicle. This can then be amortized and used as a basis for fair cost calculations in the case of termination or change in direction. In the event that a service must be stopped or significantly reworked, the supplier can ask the buyer to pay off the remaining portion of that investment. This works much like a kill fee, and it is the same principle used in the termination for convenience clause.

Although establishing a termination for convenience provision may seem to benefit the supplier, it usually benefits the buyer. It is much fairer than signing a contract in which it is impossible to change direction without invoking very large termination charges or without being forced to sign on to new long-term contracts that are not at market rates.

Another factor to consider is the close relationship between service levels and pricing. Outsourcing is fundamentally a step-change vehicle, and a reduction in price is one of the main reasons companies want to outsource. Most people think of price as differing from service levels, but price really is one of the key metrics of the relationship. It is, perhaps, the most important metric in that it drives behavior, both on the buyer side and the supplier side.

Buyers use metrics to set the level of performance the supplier must meet. The penalties or consequences usually attached to metrics define much of the risk of the supplier. Objective service levels measure the results and work to the advantage of both the suppliers and buyers. When adequate metrics are in place and used by the buyer as the tool to manage the relationship, they provide the supplier with freedom to make changes and improvements to the process. Many of these changes will be for the supplier's benefit and will result in lower costs and increased supplier profits. The buyer should not object as long as it continues to receive the results it purchased.

**Price by Measurable Results**
Usually both parties are better off structuring pricing by results rather than by some component. This focuses both parties on the real advantages of outsourcing and does not allow pricing to dictate how the service must be performed. Having said this, if a fractured process is being outsourced (as is often the case in IT), it probably will not be possible

to structure fair pricing by an easy-to-understand business result. This is because the results will be too varied and will not be controlled completely by the supplier. In these cases, it is better to price by cost drivers. That is why pricing for many data processing outsourcing agreements is often set per desktop, per service call or other pricing mechanism that is closely linked to the elements that drive the cost.

A common mistake that buyers make is to agree to pay a premium on the services with the understanding that the premium is to compensate the supplier for some undefined service that the buyer will need in the future.

This is what happened when a buyer I know agreed to pay what amounted to a 15 percent increase in price. The buyer thought the price increase was to pay for new technology as it became available. After several years of not seeing any new investments in technology, the buyer became disenchanted, especially since other customers of the same supplier received the new technologies. The supplier, on the other hand, had conveniently forgotten that it was getting a 15 percent premium. It believed the higher price was to pay for the superior service level it believed it was providing.

The moral of this story: Buyers need to be very careful not to pay a premium for things they cannot define or measure. Paying for an undefined result often happens when buyers have some vague notions about being helped and benefits accruing to them because of the alliance with the supplier. Paying for unmeasurable results is to agree to pay a premium for "better customer service"—without being able to measure the level of satisfaction.

Undefined results and unmeasurable results are the same coin with different sides. As an example, a buyer might agree to pay an additional sum of money because the supplier will do asset management. But, without developing metrics that will determine whether or not the asset management is actually happening, the buyer may pay for something it does not actually receive. Basically, the buyer has only defined the scope of the work; it has not defined the metrics.

In an HR example, let's say that the defined process and scope are that the supplier trains the buyer's employees. Without metrics, the buyer will not be able to determine whether people have been trained or if the training has been effective.

The reality is that the benefits the buyer thinks it is purchasing seldom occur unless they have been identified and are measurable. This is not surprising. I mentioned earlier that we get what we inspect—not what we expect. In such an instance, the buyer stands the risk of not getting value for its money.

The greatest potential problem for a buyer is to agree to a pricing structure where it will pay for results that have not been defined. I am constantly amazed by how often buyers are dissatisfied that they are not getting a particular result, only to find that the result was never defined in the contract.

(Supposedly, it was understood by both sides, but no one wrote it down.) As we have already seen, one of the supplier's leverages is that it only does what it is told; this usually takes the form of a written contract.

It is common sense. Buyers beware: if a metric is not defined, you won't get it. If you can't define it, you don't know when you have it. If you don't define it, you should not pay for it.

***Adjusting price through negotiations.*** Outsourcing participants agree to 10-year-long deals (or longer) because they believe they can renegotiate at any time. Wise buyers should have modest expectations of what negotiations can accomplish. Typically, buyers who agree to long-term contracts are in for a nasty surprise when they discover they don't have the ability to break a contract without considerable expense and inconvenience. They only have the ability to mutually agree on a new price. That agreement implies that the supplier will agree with the buyer, but the supplier will not be inclined to do so unless it gets concessions from the buyer.

Suppliers tend to take advantage of buyers that are in a situation where changes to service levels or pricing conditions are needed but the buyer has no ability to break the contract. Suppliers can use that situation to obtain a much higher price than they otherwise would get. A buyer is much better off in a shorter-term relationship.

***Adjusting price through benchmarking.*** In long-term contracts that do not offer opportunities to re-bid the services on a frequent basis, regular benchmarking can be a helpful vehicle for both supplier and buyer to be able to see where costs and performance lie in comparison to other businesses. When you benchmark (the current price, unencumbered by investment), you compare how well someone else is doing for that service elsewhere in the world or in the country.

Most buyers find this tool difficult to use and of limited benefit in negotiating lower rates. The supplier can easily challenge benchmarks, and even the most generic services can be made to appear unique. Since the market provides the only reliable benchmark, the lack of competition implicit in most benchmarking scenarios places the buyer at a significant disadvantage. Only when the buyer is able to go to the market will it achieve the kind of negotiating leverage that can bring price down.

However, there are some cases in which the investment required to establish the outsourcing relationship is so substantial that a longer than optimal contract is necessary.

Benchmarking may be a helpful mechanism in these cases to adjust pricing as the contract progresses. If this is the case, buyers should establish a detailed benchmarking methodology as part of the contract and designate a third-party arbitrator to rule, should there be a disagreement.

Potentially, benchmarking is also inequitable to the supplier in two ways. First, it does not reflect the investment that the supplier had to put into the relationship. Although it gets put back into the unit cost over a period of time, it does not take into account the specific investments made by that supplier in that specific situation.

Secondly, every supplier claims that it customizes the products to fit its unique situation with the buyer. Both of these arguments of suppliers have merit; but both together mean that it is very difficult to use benchmarking to adjust pricing in an outsourcing deal.

Other organizations may have achieved superior cost positions; however, it is important to note the mechanism that caused those organizations to achieve the results. If another organization used large capital investments, for example, a similar strategy may have to be considered if the same results are to be achieved. In these instances, the interests of the supplier must be taken into consideration. The supplier will need a sufficient time and profit margin to recoup any investment, or it must be able to leverage the investment across other customers from which it will recoup its investment.

To expect investment from the supplier without providing for its economic interests is unfair and highly unlikely to work.

***Adjusting price for cost of living (COLA).*** Suppliers often attempt to attach cost-of-living adjustments to their pricing. COLA can be defined as a basket of goods. It might, for example, include an increase in real estate, while the cost of the outsourced process is not affected by real estate costs. Another example would be—in a highly labor-dependent process—that the cost of labor may be rising or falling. If the supplier has control over that, it may have some ability to use different labor (going offshore, for instance) rather than adjusting price through COLA. A supplier should be able to compensate for any increases in cost through productivity improvements.

COLA is an effective mechanism, but it tends to be abused and tends to play in the suppliers' favor. The supplier is, in effect, trying to adjust the relationship for inflation and implies that there is no improvement (in economies of scale, for instance) that should accrue to the buyer, because of inflation.

Normally, when a cost-of-living adjustment is necessary, it is a good indication that the contract term is too long. The parties ought to reduce the service agreement to a point where the supplier isn't too much at risk for COLA. Obviously, the shorter the contract, the better. You can normally judge where inflation is going over a two or three-year term; a 10-year contract would place the supplier in more risk. As pointed out previously, the participants should move away from longer-term contracts to long-term relationships with short-term contracts.

***Paying for additional contributions.*** Additional business contributions may be described as the supplier taking "fine-tuning" actions that fall within the primary service provision. The value created through additional contribution must be compensated by a different means, separate and apart from the pricing of the outsourced process.

# THE PRICE OF GOLD

I have consistently found it is a mistake to pay extra for services in the expectation that the supplier will add undefined value over the life of the relationship. In these instances, what usually happens is that any premium that is paid becomes quickly appropriated by the supplier as its right and fails to act as the intended motivator. This, in return, causes the buyer to be resentful and starts a downward spiral, which benefits neither party.

My advice is to negotiate a fair price for the outsourced services, commensurate with the quality you expect to receive. The buyer should then expect to pay for new initiatives either through direct payments as the supplier participates in them, or in a value-sharing agreement in proportion to the risk that is undertaken by the supplier in providing the service. Innovative incentives can ensure that the supplier will definitely become a valuable resource in creating value.

The buyer should not pay extra for core services to pay for the additional initiatives. The supplier appropriates any premium for core services as its right. If the buyer overpays the supplier, the incentive to achieve goals will be lost, or the payment for the contribution may not be adequate for the process.

It is best for both parties to track such additional contributions as separate initiatives because, in order to make the contributions, the supplier may need to make business investments and add resources to a process. These can be paid for as the process goes along or on a contingency basis if the goal is met.

If a supplier's resources are put at risk, the buyer will pay more on a contingency basis. That is only fair, for reward follows risk. If the buyer pays for the supplier's time and effort in the primary area with an adequate profit margin, then any bonus associated with a successful impact on the business ought to be more modest.

I ran into a situation in which an outsourcing customer agreed that a portion of its price was to pay for new application development projects that it could ask the supplier to do without increasing its cost. Three years into the contract, the buyer asked the supplier to develop several applications under the original terms.

First, the supplier claimed that the type of application development was outside the scope of the contract. When this failed to deter the buyer, the supplier insisted the projects were too large to be covered under the contract.

As you might imagine, this story did not have a happy ending for either party. As this book went to print, this point was in litigation.

***Contingency (incentive-based) pricing.*** Contingency pricing is risk sharing based on results. And the greater the risk, the greater the payoff. At its core, it is an acceptance that a premium paid on value will be paid to the supplier only if the expected event or result occurs, despite whether other people in the company become involved or whether external events intervene to prevent the full value.

Incentive-based pricing is a movement primarily driven by suppliers facing intense pricing pressures. In the data processing field, the major established suppliers (led by EDS, IBM, and CSC) have faced a host of new entrants in the market that are competing on price. The established suppliers have looked for ways to improve their positions on the value chain and yet protect the pricing to which they (and their shareholders) have been accustomed. Their marketing efforts center on the additional value they believe they have been delivering. But buyers have taken a "show me" attitude.

Pricing based on added value is not yet widely practiced in outsourcing; and buyers have, up to now, been reluctant to embrace it. Their resistance stems from the problem of how to measure the extra value contribution that is being made. Difficulty in measuring is centered on the fact that the value is often beyond the business process that is being performed by the supplier. Value that the suppliers believe they are impacting may, for example, be associated with time to market, increased quality, improved buyer satisfaction, and shorter cycle time. They want their pricing to reflect their impact on these things. Buyers, however, don't want to pay a premium on core services unless the supplier can prove it delivered these extra values.

The fact is that the outsourcing suppliers' claims on impacting value have held little credibility to buyers. A supplier could actually deliver on what it said with value still not being created because of external circumstances or even the buyer's internal changes. The buyers' reluctance to accept this structure is centered on the difficulty in determining who is responsible for making the extra value (or profit) happen.

This structure was seen in the petrochemical industry for a while. It was able to achieve risk-sharing vehicles in which early development and target prices were established for the development of deep-sea oil-drilling equipment. If the suppliers (custom builders) were able to bring the projects in for less than the target pricing and total cost, they split the savings on a pro-rated basis.

I also have been associated with setting up similar situations, where the supplier outsourced desktop maintenance and the buyer maintained the cost of the facilities and equipment. Incentives were set up so that a measurement was done on total cost of ownership per desktop, including the cost of hardware, software, maintenance and the people. An incentive (sharing in savings) was paid to the supplier if the total cost was driven down.

Despite the difficulties associated with it, contingency pricing holds great promise as a way to share risk and adequately motivate both parties toward creating value. The following examples illustrate successful instances where contingency pricing succeeded.

***Contingency-based relationship of JCPenney and CF Data.*** In this relationship, JCPenney's goal was to improve its check collection rate. It determined through research that it needed to make a significant investment in new technology so it could reengineer the check collection process. In addition, it had to adopt new policies and procedures and train its staff. The supplier, CF Data, agreed to take on risk and undertake much of the investment, including technology and training. The supplier actually paid more than half of the investment, and most of it was in the buyer's infrastructure.

The result of this joint effort was that the percentage of bad debt collected increased by a factor of 20 percent—a clear win for JCPenney. The payoff for CF Data was twofold. First, it was able to improve its efficiency in collecting checks and also lowered the cost per collection. The supplier pocketed this savings instead of passing it on to JCPenney. Second, JCPenney provided more collections business to CF Data based on its successful results.

In this win-win situation, the supplier was able to achieve the premium. The buyer avoided investment yet achieved the desired result of reduced bad debt. This even became a central plank in CF Data's marketing efforts to acquire relationships with other buyers, and it has differentiated the company in the marketplace.

***Contingency-Based CTC Communications.*** In this outsourcing contract, CTC retained International Network Services (INS), now a subsidiary of Lucent Technologies, to build and install a backbone network. The goal was to establish a high-quality network quickly before its competitors implemented similar networks, thus capturing a first mover advantage by being first in the marketplace. CTC agreed to pay a substantial premium to the supplier if its difficult-to-accomplish goals were accomplished. The supplier risked losing that premium and would have to pay a penalty if it did not accomplish the goals on time. However, there also was a bonus based on the performance of the network during the first six months of use.

The result of the incentive was that the supplier delivered a world-class network much earlier than anticipated and made a substantial profit in excess of its normal fees. The payoff for CTC was that it was the first of its type of company to implement a high-quality network in its market. CTC capitalized on this first mover advantage and its gains in market share. Its stock price moved from $7 per share to $77 per share.

The real punch line here is that CTC originally rationalized this aggressive move on a risk-management basis. It looked at the contingency as an insurance policy. If it worked, the project would be brought in on time at high quality for a premium, and the amount of the premium was less than was built in for expected overruns. By preventing the overruns, the buyer paid the supplier less money.

Although CTC ended up paying the full premium, it was well worth it. The buyer's early mover advantage exceeded the premium, and it received a high-quality network, which allowed it to succeed as a business. The value that was generated and the risk that was avoided or minimized were well in excess of the incentive pay. An additional premium was associated with the supplier getting better equipment pricing for the buyer. This lowered the buyer's investment costs, and the supplier was given a portion of those savings, too.

*Gain/Share Strategy in Contingency Pricing.* Bay Networks Inc, a computer networking hardware company, wanted to motivate its supplier, Andersen Consulting, to finish a project on time and under budget. The measurement was the number of days the supplier estimated it would take to complete the project. The incentive-based deal was an agreement that both sides would assume a portion of the risk. If the project were not completed on time with an acceptable level of quality, the supplier would refund 10 percent of its price to the buyer. If the project could be completed ahead of schedule with acceptable quality, the buyer would pay the supplier a 10 percent premium.

The end result was a check from Bay Networks to Andersen Consulting for the 10 percent bonus. However, the supplier had already spent that amount of money bringing in experts to get the project done on time to avoid a 10 percent penalty.

## The Use of Co-sourcing

Although EDS, who service marked and coined the term "co-sourcing," recognizes that the marketplace and media generally describe it as a friendly collaboration, it is not the definition EDS had in mind. Co-sourcing, per EDS, is very focused on business performance and is directed toward improving the business metrics under which a company operates. A co-sourcing arrangement involves a major piece of consultancy work taking place in reengineering the business process. In co-sourcing, the supplier goes in on an enterprise-wide level and becomes a partner in planning an organizational transformation or even an entirely new business.

In co-sourcing, there generally is a series of projects with limited duration, which achieve a particular goal—a reduction in overall cost structure, or a cycle time improvement, for example. In addition to these projects, the participants sign an outsourcing agreement, which is to run a series of processes (often IT). The co-sourcing arrangement (and the supplier's compensation) is focused on the successful completion of the reengineering projects.

The whole idea of co-sourcing is to get the best out of both organizations. It is a total joint effort. While the supplier will take the lead on certain aspects of processes in the relationship, ultimately the leadership has to come from the buyer. In co-sourcing, the buyer's core processes, as well as its important but non-core processes are involved; in this way, co-sourcing differs from all other outsourcing alliances.

There are two notable examples of co-sourcing—the Rolls-Royce Aerospace Group and Kellwood Company deals with EDS. (These deals are also good examples of contingency-based pricing).

*The Rolls-Royce Aerospace Group and EDS Contract.* The objectives of the Rolls-Royce Aerospace Group in England were not focused on cost containment but, rather, were concentrated on its customers' needs—speeding up innovation, producing new engines faster and adapting them to more airframes in a shorter period of time. Additionally, Rolls-Royce sought to accomplish globalization with the use of common systems. The challenge for EDS was to support the redesigning of the Rolls-Royce processes and to invest in IT to implement the new processes without showing a substantial impact on revenues generated.

In the Rolls-Royce "Better Performance Faster" program, EDS agreed to take as compensation for the business process reengineering an incentive-based reward, thus putting at risk its significant investment. As a risk-sharing partner, Rolls-Royce would pay EDS for the impact it made. The predefined premium would cover not only the cost of the activity but would also reward the activity at a higher level. The occurrence of value would come through step changes in which specific results would be achieved. EDS was paid its bonus after lowering operating costs and improving quality.

*The Kellwood Company and EDS Contract.* Kellwood is a U.S. apparel company with products spread over 180 clothing labels. Its objective was to put in joint processes and efficiencies for all its consolidations and acquisitions. EDS contracted to manage the nine existing IT services, develop a new

IT structure, and solve year 2000 problems. The role of EDS was to reengineer Kellwood's supply chain management process. This included targeting new suppliers, managing the new suppliers, and handling the logistics and warehouse functions. The fee to EDS was paid out of savings accomplished through its manufacturing improvements.

A value-added piece of both of these transactions is EDS's relationship with A. T. Kearney, a component that is embedded in EDS's major deals. Kearney brings all competencies together in leadership strategies and high-level problem solving to one or more multi-disciplinary teams working to accomplish the reengineering. In the Rolls-Royce deal, for example, multi-disciplinary teams are composed of Kearney's best-practice consultants, Rolls-Royce business executives and EDS systems experts. It is these teams that work concurrently to redesign the processes and the new systems.

## The Conflict and Five Issues Inherent in Contingency Pricing and Co-Sourcing

The theory of determining fair compensation in a contingency contract is that the compensation is a payment based on successful completion of projects or upon profit generated from anticipated results. In implementation, however, many issues cause conflict. Buyers typically want suppliers to "act like a partner" and make investments. Suppliers, in return, want to be guaranteed their fair share of the profits resulting from their investment. Buyers, though, are typically unwilling to pay a premium if the supplier does not take any risk. The suppliers don't want to go out on a limb that may not be strong enough to hold them.

Most buyers come to the negotiating table arguing that they do not want to pay anything or that they want the supplier to take more risk than it has agreed to. Buyers want suppliers to put a portion or all of their costs at stake and be paid only on results. The suppliers take the position that they will undertake to perform the series of initiatives at modest or no profit and hope that they will be allowed a larger share. By basing their profit on the results and, therefore, taking risk, they believe they should be paid a larger amount if the results are there. Obviously, these diverse viewpoints create friction.

*Issue 1: The amount of supplier risk.* Clearly, there is a relationship to the total amount of profits that can be made and the amount of risk that must be undertaken. The negotiation process involves solving problems in determining how much risk the supplier will take. Typically, this varies from a position where the supplier pays for all the activities and receives compensation only on the results, to a position where both parties agree to share costs with some of the supplier's profits dependent on that. A wise buyer will examine what is really at risk. Suppliers typically take the position that they want their costs covered.

*Issue 2: What constitutes "cost."* The suppliers' desire to have their costs covered brings in another problem—how to determine what is "cost." Should overhead and out-of-pocket expenses be included in cost, for instance?

The issue of cost-plus comes into play and is very problematic. What constitutes cost is very much open to dispute—particularly with multinational companies, where there are corporate overhead, cross-subsidization, and tax minimization strategies.

*Issue 3: Who is responsible for the result (increase in profits).* Suppliers receive their compensation based on either a percentage of profits of the company, a contingent payment and/or a cash payment resulting from successful completion of the project, or an arbitrary amount of money that is, in effect, a bonus payment. The compensation would be paid either upon successful completion of the project or upon the anticipated results generated from profit. Suppliers, therefore, must be able to demonstrate that they are responsible for the increase in profit. That can prove very difficult.

The problem is that there are a number of other things, besides what the supplier is doing, that impact profit, such as technology solutions, economic conditions, regulations or happenings within the buyer's company. The supplier must be able to draw a relationship from its tasks to the result. A key issue in negotiation, then, goes beyond a description of what the supplier will do. It becomes necessary for the supplier to specifically demonstrate how its contribution definitely impacts the results.

*Issue 4: How to fairly measure the contribution (value).* Contribution means that the participants agree to share the value that has been created, rather than profits. This poses the problems of defining what the value is and how to measure it objectively. Then it must be determined how much should be shared with the supplier. This is, essentially, the same problem that exists with profits—buyers and suppliers have different viewpoints on how to define value. Value is difficult to measure and, as with profits, it is necessary to understand the percentage of the supplier's impact on results.

Buyers typically prefer to measure contribution as the actual impact made on the business; they pay only if there is an increase in value or profit. Suppliers typically prefer to be compensated on successful completion of the projects, implying that value was created if the business then works with the desired results. It is easier to measure whether a project is completed than to measure whether or not value is created (that is, whether profits go up or down because of those projects).

*Issue 5: The duration of the reward.* The participants must also decide how long those profits will be shared. In an efficient market, it can be expected that competitors will match innovations over time; therefore, the value would change and no longer merit the same reward. Value tends to have a short life; the sharing of that value should also be over a short period of time.

Risk management is part of everyday life in companies today. If handled wisely, it is not a gamble on a venture with an uncertain outcome. Risk, used within structured contexts, is a calculated maneuver toward a highly profitable and successful business.

Through experience in structuring these alliances, I find that contingency-based pricing is not always appropriate, nor can it be accomplished in all situations. For risk-based structures to be successful, the potential alliance participants must do four things: 1) have an objective means of measuring results; 2) identify the components that will accomplish those results; 3) identify which party will perform each task or initiative to accomplish the results; and 4) determine the costs to accomplish those results and which party will pay for them. Unless all four of these components are in place, it would be unwise to structure an outsourcing alliance around contingency pricing. If, on the other hand, these components can be determined, the parties would then be in a position to adequately negotiate such a deal. When all of these components have been negotiated, the vulnerability of unforeseen risk will have been eliminated from the alliance.

Whatever process you consider for outsourcing, you will want to remember the following advice. The key to establishing a price is to describe adequately the scope of the services you are purchasing. Be able to measure objectively the results you expect and establish a pricing structure which communicates more than just cost.

# THE PRICE OF GOLD

The use of contingent pricing in outsourcing is still a new and relatively untried tool. It most closely parallels alchemy because it holds great promise to generate wealth or value where none existed before. However, just as the experiments of the early alchemists sometimes ended in failure, so too have some outsourcing experiments not worked out well. There have been numerous blind alleys.

## Chapter 8

# GOLD PURIFIERS AND INHIBITORS

*Ninety-nine percent of success is
built on former failure.*
—Charles F. Kettering, founder of
General Motors

Religious groups in the Middle Ages believed that the medieval alchemists' art was of the occult. So the alchemists decided to write their formulas in riddles and code because the knowledge they had acquired was not intended for everyone. Silver was referred to as "The White Queen," and precious gold was called "The Red Man." The mysterious words in their books were necessary, not only because they thought that the value of gold would lessen if everyone could make it, but also because they felt a need to protect their work from the church and other inhibitors of their operations.

As we consider how to make use of the modern alchemy of outsourcing, we need to understand some behaviors and common practices that can ensure or inhibit the creation of value.

This chapter explains these issues from the viewpoint of both the supplier and the buyer. Without this knowledge, a new entrant into the outsourcing field is like an alchemist who hopes to make a fortune but who is without the chemicals and the equipment necessary for the process.

### A Supplier's Prerequisites for Success

The most common inhibitor to success is the supplier management team's lack of understanding of the nature of outsourcing. A new supplier may take the attitude that it will sign up customers and then make the necessary investment in economies of scale, process improvements, and other leverage components. Because outsourcing is a relatively high-risk venture (one that entails significant switching costs for buyers entering it for the first time), buyers spend a significant amount of time reassuring themselves that the supplier can, in fact, do the work.

The first thing buyers pay close attention to is references. Most buyers want to see references from at least three other companies that have already used the supplier's service successfully. Second, most buyers want to see a strong balance sheet with adequate capital to overcome any potential problems that might occur over a sustained period of time.

Buyers also look for evidence of a well-articulated, superior process. This is often transmitted by the supplier through a well-organized, methodical sales process that demonstrates due diligence. Suppliers not possessing a well-honed methodology usually find their prospects jilting them at the altar. Buyers want to be assured of a supplier's commitment to high quality. Increasingly, this takes the form of looking for real metrics with meaningful consequences attached.

A potential supplier entrant must have these elements in place before it approaches the market. Recognizing the opportunity in outsourcing and offering a service simply are not enough. Putting these components into place can require significant capital and creative entry strategies. The expansion of IBM Global Services into the Australian market is a good example of how to do this. To be successful in that marketplace, IBM recognized that it would have to secure sufficient economies of scale and high-profile references. Even the enormous credibility that IBM already enjoyed needed to be supplemented with other strengths. So it formed an outsourcing joint venture with Telstra and Lend Lease Corp., two large Australian companies. Success resulted.

Because they lack some of the necessary marketing characteristics, many new supplier entrants find it necessary to provide additional incentives to their first three customers. These might take the form of equity participation, cash infusions or other valuable incentives. Most new entrants are forced to secure significant financial backing in the form of parent grantees, joint ventures or venture capital. Furthermore, they often make significant investments in building economies of scale and in developing methodologies and superior process design before they ever attract a customer.

The need for these factors to come together in a hurry has driven many new entrants to adopt an acquisition model in which they seek to purchase existing outsourcing supplier companies that already are active in the niche the entrant wishes to penetrate. A variation is that it may purchase software or consulting companies that already have developed the expertise or economies of scale.

A supplier can establish all the factors described above and still need another component for success. Aspiring entrants must learn the perils of the outsourcing sales model. The first thing that the sales team must learn has been well illustrated by the Italian political philosopher, Machiavelli. He wrote that there is nothing more difficult or dangerous than to introduce a new order of things. He was referring to instituting a new monarchy and system of government. It is precisely the same issues that the modern outsourcing supplier faces as it seeks to wrest a process away from an internal department of the buyer's organization. Even though the supplier can do the process better and cheaper, the employees of the buyer's department will generate significant resistance because their jobs probably will be at stake.

The virulent resistance put up by the buyer organization as it struggles to repel this unwanted invasion often shocks new entrants. It requires a sales force skilled in this type of sale, backed up by a management team committed to the expense and effort that is required. The significant sales cost forces the would-be supplier's management to be selective in the prospects pursued. This adds another skill to the list of those required in the supplier's management team—one that they typically lack if they are not already experienced in outsourcing sales.

Most successful new entrants develop dedicated sales teams that sell outsourcing exclusively. In most cases, these sales teams require different skills, different compensation plans and a specialized approach to sales management. In my experience, a failure to develop such a team almost always ends in disaster. Even AT&T Solutions, which had huge resources, unquestioned technical competence, impressive economies of scale and great financial stability, still created a separate subsidiary with a dedicated outsourcing sales staff in its successful bid to create its own outsourcing business.

Selling outsourcing is different from selling equipment or selling consulting. Many of today's aspiring suppliers come from companies that already provide services or products to an established industry. Since they already participate in the industry, these companies often have the makings of the needed leverage and the industry acceptance that is needed to become a successful outsourcing supplier. Their senior management recognizes the potential opportunity and announces to the world the company's desire to enter this new market segment.

Nevertheless, they often fail to anticipate who in the buying organization has made the decision to outsource. All outsourcing decisions come from the top down. In most other types of relationships, the sale is made to department heads, engineers, or middle management; in outsourcing, however, a decision to purchase is always made one or two levels above the department whose work is to be outsourced.

The new outsourcing supplier already has strong relationships with an existing clientele, so it calls on executives it already knows and, in effect, offers to put its old clients out of business. Understandably, this causes the old clientele to feel betrayed. In fact, it often causes them to stop doing business with the supplier. As initially only a small percentage of the new supplier's old customers will convert to outsourcing, this can destroy the supplier's existing business. If the approach does not have this effect, it may at least cause significant internal resistance within the customer's company when it comes to supporting this new market.

I have seen this pattern repeated several times. It explains why the outsourcing industry has had such problems building effective consulting practices. It also explains why, when an existing consulting practice is acquired, there may be problems integrating this into the mainstream business. The two entities are natural enemies and work to undermine each other. The supplier cannot use the same sales people to sell outsourcing to call on department heads; it just does not work. Consulting is a sale to a department head or technical expert; outsourcing is an executive sale. New entrants often find that it is not enough just to develop a new sales force; they often have to establish separate subsidiaries (as AT&T and IBM have done.)

As explained in Chapter 7, a supplier's bundling of prices and services creates confusion as to what is being bought and allows an unscrupulous supplier to claim that certain activities or results were not involved in the original deal. Prices must be easily understood by both parties and directly attached to the services being provided. Adequate backup evidence when presenting an invoice to a buyer is an important practice. One-line-item bills are an abomination, though they are the industry standard. A detailed services invoice will help the buyer to understand what it has bought so that it can reallocate its costs to the end users. Additionally, this is good account management practice because it permits the supplier to communicate exactly what drives a particular cost.

## A Buyer's Prerequisites for Success

From the buyer's perspective there is an equally large number of dysfunctional behaviors and assumptions to be overcome. The first, and most fundamental, mistake a buyer typically makes is forgetting that it traded an internal infrastructure, with its myriad personnel and technical issues, for a business relationship with the supplier. Problems occur when the buyer continues to try to manage the process and does not allow the more expert supplier to deal with how the results will be provided.

The key to this issue of management is to keep the relationship focused on the main issues that drive the outsourcing process. I advise buyers not to permit day-to-day minutiae to intrude on their outsourcing relationships and to address issues as they arise in the light of whether or not they impact value. Questions that can help a buyer understand which issues are important enough to fight for include:

How much will it cost my company?

How much will it cost the supplier to resolve the problem?

Does the problem offer an opportunity to create contributions?

The first thing a buyer and supplier must do is put a businessperson in charge of the outsourcing process. Allowing a technical person to manage the relationship can doom it from the start (especially if the buyer's technical person comes from or has expertise in the infrastructure that is being outsourced). A businessperson can understand the overall context in which the relationship takes place and is able to take a balanced approach to issues. A technical person is more likely to feel threatened by the supplier and tends to focus only on the technical points.

Suppliers believe in the old playground trading-card theory—I'll trade you two marbles for one McGwire card. They find it a lot easier to barter than to resolve issues that have a monetary value. A buyer should take advantage of that. The supplier's technical manager usually fails to understand the change in the relationship and continues to manage the function as though it were still part of the buyer's organization.

Another key behavioral practice for the buyer is not to sweat the small stuff. Focus, instead, on major issues—on how value is being transacted, for example. Winning every battle or every issue is not the strategy to use when working with an outside organization. Battles should be chosen wisely. There needs to be some fairness about the relationship; there should be something in it for both parties. The supplier's agenda should not run the relationship; it should be run with the buyer's business objectives in mind. But a buyer who asks its supplier to make investments should take the supplier's costs into consideration.

A common phenomenon in outsourcing is for some suppliers to attempt to achieve their profits by moving functions that were originally intended by the buyer to be in the scope of service and then claim they are not a part of that service. This phenomenon most often occurs when the buyer has not adequately defined the scope of the outsourced services or when the two parties agree to enter into a contract and then define the scope and service levels after the contract has begun. In the latter case, the supplier is in a strong position to reposition the service boundaries to maximize its revenue.

Another common mistake made by buyers is not to address important buyer issues as a strategy to preserve harmony, hoping the supplier will get to them. Invariably, the supplier simply will ignore the unapprised issues. A buyer needs to realize that, by not addressing issues important to its company, the supplier receives an implicit message that those issues are not important and don't have value. Relationships are built on precedents, so it is critical not to set poor ones.

The supplier's "training" of the buyer is vital but can be an inhibitor to the success of the relationship. Say, for example, that a manipulative supplier employs a hard-nosed account manager whose job is to tell the customer "no" repeatedly and that the supplier then replaces him six months to a year later with an account manager who goes a little easier on the buyer. The result would be that the buyer would feel more comfortable with the new account manger and—voila!—the buyer has been trained to accept a lower level of performance than was originally anticipated.

Buyers should be aware that this phenomenon works both ways. Buyers establish a climate and level of expectation, to which the suppliers will adapt. An environment of accountability and fairness breeds professionalism. An environment with little or no accountability can lead to poor performance or, worse, allow an unscrupulous supplier to redefine the scope of its services so it can charge extra for functions that were originally part of the contract.

Each side needs to realize that, although being trained is a positive and necessary step, the best practice is to deal with issues immediately and in a positive manner. Both parties need to train each other in how to work.

As explained previously, a buyer should not expect that paying a premium price on the outsourced process entitles it to additional contribution. The supplier will regard whatever it is paid as being fair. A buyer must be prepared to pay extra compensation for extra services.

It is important early in the relationship for the buyer not to establish the precedent of accepting supplier invoices without adequate backup. An invoice without adequate backup really is not an invoice and never should be processed. It is also good practice for the buyer then to reallocate to its consuming departments or entities the true overall costs of the services being provided by the supplier.

### Conflict Resolution

Inevitably, a time of mutual antagonism will come in an outsourcing relationship; or a buyer may ask its supplier to do something it is not prepared to do. Both parties need to remember that their relationship is a business transaction and that all discussions should be civil. When discussions degenerate into personal attacks, it is inevitable that the individuals involved on both sides will have to be removed from the process.

Those crazy "ates"—escalate, arbitrate, humiliate, mitigate, terminate and litigate—can be avoided or, at least, reduced by having a businessperson in charge of the relationship. A businessperson will view the other side as an asset that potentially provides ever-increasing returns. I know sometimes personalities don't mix and that one or both sides place the wrong people in positions of influence, but it is the buyer's obligation to ensure that the wrong people do not remain in the outsourcing relationship. From the supplier's perspective, it must constantly prove that the current structure is equitable, fair and consistent with the value proposition at hand.

A good way to avoid this situation is for the relationship manager to try to adopt the perspective that his or her counterpart on the supplier's side is a potential asset for both companies. This asset becomes a valuable tool that provides a variety of solutions to the many business problems that face the organization.

In our world, it is best for kings to talk to kings, for queens to talk to queens, and for pawns to talk to pawns. Buyers need to pay attention to the corporate hierarchy and try to talk to a compatriot at their level. A buyer should never overuse its executives to handle minor problems. An executive is like an atomic bomb—the threat of using one is very powerful, but the side effects of exploding one for a trivial cause can be disastrous. Intervention by an executive can be useful at times, but executives should not get involved (especially in day-to-day operations) too frequently, as it diminishes their effectiveness in making an impact on the other party when their power really needs to be felt.

I have developed a simple document to use as a tool in addressing conflict resolution. This tool can be used for any number of situations or issues, and it focuses on the following points.

## Issue Management

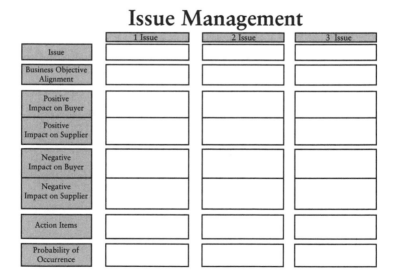

| | 1 Issue | 2 Issue | 3 Issue |
|---|---|---|---|
| Issue | | | |
| Business Objective Alignment | | | |
| Positive Impact on Buyer | | | |
| Positive Impact on Supplier | | | |
| Negative Impact on Buyer | | | |
| Negative Impact on Supplier | | | |
| Action Items | | | |
| Probability of Occurrence | | | |

(1) Issue: Each conflict or issue is identified at the top of the page.

(2) Business objective: What business objectives are the people who are in conflict trying to achieve? Defining the objectives may serve to identify the root cause of the conflict. If neither side can agree initially on what the goal is, that is likely to be the cause of the problem.

(3) Positive impact: Impact can be described in dollars, market share or system performance. It usually becomes the primary metric of the business objective.

(4) Negative impact on the buyer: What is the cost of not taking a particular action? Will the buyer lose market share? Will its business be negatively affected in other ways?

(5) Negative impact on the supplier: What would happen to the supplier if the project were not implemented? Obviously, there would be a possible revenue loss. Would there be other negative impacts and long-term effects on the relationship? If so, what could they be? The discussions elicited by these sorts of questions will raise even more questions that are germane to the subject of conflict resolution.

(6) Action items: Identify the actions that need to be taken (including by whom and when) in order to resolve the conflict. Also identify the estimated costs (in time and labor hours or days) needed to accomplish these actions. These can be identified in rough order of magnitude. This gives perspective on what it will take to resolve the issue, shows who will need

to do what, estimates costs, and provides an indirect measurement of the investment in the solution.

(7) Probability of occurrence: This is an estimate provided independently (often by secret ballot) from both sides as to what the chances are that both sides can resolve the issue.

Essentially, the conflict resolution tool gives a framework to the discussion, creating common vantage points so that both sides can work together toward a mutually acceptable solution. It is hoped that by the end of the discussion, both sides will realize that they can succeed only together and that, if divided, they are likely to fail.

One last word about a crazy "ate"— don't manipulate. If you do, problems inevitably will escalate and come back to haunt you.

### Nurturing the Relationship

An often overlooked impediment to value creation is the human side of outsourcing. Long-term relationships require that friendships and respect be developed and sustained over long periods of time. Many ignore the necessity to tend to these relationships and, in so doing, reap an unintentional whirlwind of distrust and destructive behavior on the part of the account executives and their teams.

As a general philosophy, both parties should endeavor to make their counterparts heroes. A buyer should find ways to make the supplier's account manager look good for the benefit of the buyer's manager (but without allowing the supplier's account manager to get away with actions that are detrimental to the buyer). Similarly, a supplier should take actions to make its counterpart shine, for the supplier's management is an essential part of the process. If the parties don't make the effort to do this, animosity may be allowed to fester and build, with predictable consequences.

Incentives can be a helpful way to build this bonding by allowing the account executive to demonstrate that the relationship is worth investing in because it has the potential for additional profit. Efforts in "stretching" one's organization ought to be rewarded. Being able to apply incentives intelligently can have a profound effect and lead to a high return on a company's investment.

It is important for the parties to build institutional, as well as personal, relationships. Deals are often structured by executives who later may leave the organization and be replaced by individuals with no knowledge of the original relationship or deal that was made. The new executives inevitably want to bring in their own structure. The high turnover rate for executives is one of the most profound problems in outsourcing. In the IT arena alone, CIO turnover occurs approximately every 18 months. Since most outsourcing deals are for a duration of from three to 10 years, at a minimum one must expect to go through at least two CIOs. Logic, therefore, dictates that, in order to make these relationships work, they must be between institutions as well as between individuals.

My experience with this phenomenon is that, where management turnover is detrimental to the relationship, one or both parties failed to establish adequate metrics that demonstrate the value of the relationship. Often metrics are in place, but they only deal with the technical performance or are diagnostic. They do not illustrate any additional value that the supplier has brought. Business-oriented metrics are designed to do this. Where both parties are able to point to ongoing value creation, the relationship almost never is in trouble.

# Chapter 9

## From the Lab to the Shop Floor

*"In war, the stronger overcomes the weaker.
In business, the stronger imparts strength to the
weaker. If you wish to prosper,
let your customer prosper."*
— Frederick Bastiat

What separates alchemy from true science is the ability to repeat an experiment or phenomenon again and again. What separates engineering from science is the act of implementing principles in a practical application. An engineer is most interested in a phenomenon or set of principles if they hold potential for some practical use in life or in business.

Being more of an engineer than a scientist, I want to assist readers of this book to apply outsourcing's principles in their own businesses in a successful manner. I seek to assist readers, if you will, in becoming budding outsourcing engineers. So, don your hard hat, and let me show you how to apply the information I have shared thus far.

**Choosing the Best Approach to an Alliance**

As the outsourcing industry has evolved over the past decade, its shape has changed; it has found new uses and built new structures, becoming even more responsive to market needs. Relationships between buyers and suppliers of outsourcing services have turned the corner and go far beyond reducing costs. They have recognized outsourcing's fundamental usefulness in meeting the goals of business process reengineering and increased shareholder value. Outsourcing alliances with those goals are built on a foundation of teamwork, collaboration and co-functioning.

There are several different kinds of outsourcing in the marketplace. The approach or vehicle choice to outsourcing is vital, for it will go far in determining the structure by which the relationship will be defined and controlled.

There are three primary types of outsourcing vehicles. Not surprisingly, there is a lot of debate as to which of these is superior.

*The Single-Source Approach.* Here, a buyer contracts for all or most of the services in a given area to be provided by a single supplier. This is the most traditional of outsourcing methods and has the strongest historical precedent. It is also the approach most often pushed by suppliers—no doubt in hope of being that single source. There are positive and negative aspects to this method of operation.

In a single-source environment, there is little price competition because there is also little or no threat from another supplier. Therefore, over time, the motivation for the supplier to provide market pricing is less compelling, because competition and negotiation prowess is what drives price down.

Another drawback in the single-source environment is that any one company may not be world class in every area; so it is possible that a buyer would purchase lower-quality work in some aspects of the service. But this usually can be balanced by adequate performance in the area of measurement of results.

On the other hand, an advantage to the single-source approach is that, since only one supplier is involved, there will be no finger pointing between rival suppliers when the sledding gets rough. Typically, rival suppliers who operate in the same environment blame each other for problems of non-performance. The resulting rivalry and competition wastes resources, focus and energy.

As long as a single-source supplier is competent, a buyer can get adequate levels of work and competitive pricing from this approach. Typically in these situations, the supplier also would be permitted to subcontract, within certain guidelines.

***The Best-of-Breed Approach.*** Here, a buyer contracts with a number of different suppliers, allocating to each one the specific service or aspect of service for which it offers the best value. In this approach, each area being outsourced is broken up into individual services. The logistics buyer, for example, might retain one supplier to do warehouse management and another for transportation. In data processing, a buyer might have a supplier like ACS Systems, Inc. managing its data center; a company like Entech Information Services managing its desktop; AT&T Solutions managing the wide area network; and IBM managing the applications. In this best-of-breed approach, the buyer ensures superior pricing and service in the areas that each supplier is best equipped to handle.

In the data processing example, many of those companies are well positioned to provide the services that have been allocated to the other companies; so this approach introduces healthy competition. The implicit threat that the buyer might switch suppliers is always there.

However, such competition and the existence of multiple interests raise the opportunity for finger pointing or subversion of each other's services. Therefore, this approach requires strong management and very clear boundaries and service levels. Some of these negative aspects can be overcome if the buyer institutes joint service levels over one or more of the services.

***The Consortium Approach.*** In this one, a supplier brings several other suppliers together and brokers a "marriage" between them so that it can provide a potpourri of services under a single contract. The consortium solution tries to retain the benefits of the best-of-breed approach while controlling the finger pointing. (In my observation, however, the finger pointing has not yet been eliminated.) An alternative in this approach is for the supplier and buyer to form a separate corporate structure together to accomplish their goals.

The consortium is a relatively new phenomenon. In a consortium, a company orchestrates a marriage between a number of best-of-breed partners. A good example is the case of J.P. Morgan and the Pinnacle Alliance, described earlier. At the time of this writing, CSC holds the master contract and provides the data center and desktop service for Morgan while Andersen Consulting provides application support and development services, AT&T Solutions provides the wide area network, and Bell Atlantic provides the local network and wiring.

Much like the single-source methodology, the alliance approach usually removes the sources of competition. In fact, it also introduces new levels of profitability for the suppliers because the master contractor adds its own premium to all of the services.

Furthermore, where new services requiring multiple components are combined, no one supplier has enough interest to discount its services without the others discounting their services, too. It, therefore, becomes rather difficult for the buyer to achieve anything better than the standard rate from the suppliers. The buyer ends up with the double whammy of high pricing to start with and an initial premium placed for new services. The buyer does get combined accountability—which is good. But beware, because it requires strong management to pull it off.

### Buyer-Supplier Alliances

Spinouts, equity swaps and joint ventures are the three main structures used in the alliance approach; the rest of this chapter describes each of them and gives examples of their use. Companies are using them more and more because they can generate real value, thanks to the stock market.

Often implicit in these structures is the fact that a buyer will not immediately get the lowest pricing because some of the value is returned through ownership of stock, making total value higher. The buyer benefits because the newly created outsourcing company is worth more on the open market than the reduction in cost would have been. Its worth on the open market is in stock trades, and the earnings are trading at a multiple; outsourcing companies trade at a high multiple (in the 20s or higher in the U.S.). For every dollar of profit, the stock value rises, so the buyer then gets a higher value back. In addition to value in lower costs, the participants also get ownership of an asset, which has intrinsic value unto itself. Additionally, the supplier gets some price protection; it is allowed to make a higher margin than it otherwise would.

***Forming a Spinout as an Alliance Structure.*** A spinout is used where a company decides it has enough economies of scale and enough process expertise that it wants to create its own outsourcing company. It can be a bridge over troubled waters, enabling the company to divest itself of non-core activities.

In effect, the parent company creates a new subsidiary with public stock. If the executives are able to create a successful outsourcing company, that company is valued differently and often higher than the core company that created it. It allows them to attract a different source of capital to fund it. This avenue has the ability to increase the total value of the company. The spun-out company often will hire senior individuals from other outsourcing companies or buy a small outsourcing company to infuse the outsourcing knowledge into it. Following are three examples of the spinout approach.

• *Spinout of an Unwanted Unit.* Just when the outsourcing industry was enjoying explosive growth, the unique, competitive manufacturing technology unit of outsourcing supplier IBM was declared to be a non-core activity. The manufacturing unit (now called Celestica Inc.) wanted to continue building manufacturing technology for servers and workstations and participate in the global outsourcing surge; so it was acquired by a group of investors in 1996.

Originally a candidate for closure by its parent company, the spinout at the time of this writing is the number three player globally in the electronics manufacturing services market and has a sales target of $10 billion by 2001. By supplying outsourcing services to many customers and not being dependent, as it formerly was, only on its parent company, Celestica is less vulnerable to economic downturns. Lower prices to customers and acquisitions of other manufacturing spinouts have yielded a good rate of return on the capital invested in this company.

- *Entrepreneurs Spinout.* GE Information Services wanted to improve service levels of its facilities management, use performance-based pricing for bonuses and profit sharing, and refocus the attention of company management on its core business area.

To accomplish these goals, the in-house facilities management team became an outsourcing spinout, competing with other suppliers to provide support services. The maneuver was highly successful, partly due to the fact that the new company's employees retained knowledge of the parent company's culture and operations. The spun-out company, formed in 1989 and christened Facilities Plus, has since been able to introduce a management service for office relocations and a workforce service coordination that landed within the top 100 of the Inc. 500 fastest growing companies in 1994.

An even more significant benefit to this spinout is a new source of revenue through a joint venture program it devised. The company forms joint ventures with other facilities management teams to help them spin out from their original employer companies, providing the new spinouts with the necessary infrastructure and working capital that the new businesses need in order to market their services.

• *A Spinout Flying High.* Sabre, which was highly successful in the airlines industry, was spun out from American Airlines to reflect the spinout's true value in the marketplace. Although it occupied a successful niche in the travel industry before it was spun out, the group had been under pressure to innovate, using the Internet and electronic ticketing. It could not do this to full effect without becoming a separately traded company since many of its potential customers did not want their competitor (American Airlines) involved in operating one of their strategic assets. By distancing itself from its parent company, Sabre would be able to grow faster and compete for contracts with competitors of its parent company.

The technique used in this spinout structure was to do a small public offering, selling off about 20 percent of the group's stock before the rest of it was spun out. Proceeds from the public offering were first used to pay off Sabre's debt, with American Airlines reaping the major portion of the gain. This was then followed by a full spinout in which the shareholders of AMR, American's parent, received stock in Sabre.

It is interesting to note that in early 1999 Sabre formed a strategic alliance with a software solutions company to enable both organizations to further automate and streamline their customers' purchasing process with Internet-based technology.

***Using an "Equity Swap" (Cross Ownership) as an Alliance Structure.*** This is an interesting and potentially highly rewarding structure that has been utilized a number of times in the history of outsourcing. For example, in the Perot Systems/Swiss Bank outsourcing agreement, Swiss Bank agreed to a 10-year outsourcing contract with the newly formed Perot Systems in exchange for a 20 percent stake in the outsourcer.

The conditions for such a transaction arise when a large buyer desires to enter into an outsourcing alliance with a smaller supplier. In exchange for giving the supplier a significant amount of business, the large buyer's company receives equity in the supplier's company. The advantage to the buyer is that it benefits twice from the transaction – once through lower costs and a second time through participating in the value creation through the rise in the stock price. The supplier's benefits involve achieving a very large rise in revenues; access to economies of scale hitherto unachievable; market credibility through dealing with a buyer of the prestige and size of the buyer; and, finally, a significant rise in its valuation as the market takes note of its improved status.

Although this appears to be a relatively simple exchange, the opportunities for this type of structure are fairly rare, and the actual structuring of these relationships is quite complicated.

There are two common dangers associated with this type of arrangement. The most common pitfall is that the buyer tends to overpay for the outsourced services and, therefore, suffers strong dissatisfaction later in the relationship. A second and somewhat related tendency is for both the buyer and supplier to lose sight of the need to base the relationship on leverage, rather than a sudden windfall from the equity swap. This can lead both buyer and supplier into a mutually bad relationship and can cause the supplier's stock to fall, eliminating much of the value that was anticipated.

•*More than Expertise.* Another example of cross-ownership involves Telstra, Australia's largest telecommunications carrier, who joined IBM Australia and Lend Lease Corp. as an equity partner to form a new strategic alliance. The partners called the new company IBM Global Services Australia. The new venture's reason for existence is to create new joint venture opportunities in the IT outsourcing industry.

One of the joint ventures formed by this strategic alliance is a network services and solutions integration company called Advantra. All three alliance partners hold an equity stake in Advantra. Telstra owns 50 percent, IBM Australia owns 30 percent, and Lend Lease owns 20 percent. The entity these partners created has gone on to become the most successful IT outsourcing company in Australia, creating substantial value for each party.

***Forming a Joint Venture as an Alliance Structure.*** Although there are many variations to this structure, the basic theme is the same. The parties agree to own or develop a project together in return for sharing the profits together. The parties achieve economies of scale and each contributes complementary competencies. This structure is a well-established venue. It works best in industries that are going through significant change. It is a structure that necessitates both parties laying out all their cards for the other to see.

Much like the proverbial wolf in sheep's clothing, though, joint ventures often have been used to dress up outsourcing relationships so as to hide their true nature. This in itself is not a real problem if one is willing to ignore the ethical problem of deception.

Typically, the participants in joint ventures have become enamored of the vehicle and are in danger of losing sight of the leverage which is necessary to make outsourcing relationships work. By creating a jointly owned company, they may deny themselves most of the economies of scale that would otherwise be available. The implementation of improved processes also may be more difficult. Since the buyer would have more say in how the process would be deployed, this could result in eroding the supplier's process leverage.

In my experience, few outsourcing joint ventures work. An exception would be the rare case where the buyer represents a genuine entry to an outsourcing market that the supplier could not otherwise access. This typically means that the buyer has significant economies of scale or process expertise and a desire to enter the outsourcing market, but it lacks the expertise and credibility with which to make a successful entry into the outsourcing arena on its own.

Even when these conditions do exist, many of these relationships fail because an experienced supplier typically is most interested in receiving a contract for the buyer's business and is not interested in establishing the joint venture as a competitor to its own business. This does not stop suppliers from eagerly proposing these relationships. They are skilled in structuring them so that the buyer signs management contracts or subcontracts for the work. This has the effect of sucking out most, if not all, of the profits and leaving the joint venture with little, if any, profit to share among the owners.

An interesting variant of joint venture has been appearing in the market. In this approach, the supplier offers to spin out a buyer's non-core infrastructure into a 50/50 joint venture. The joint venture then sells back to the buyer the services it previously provided for itself from an internal department. This, of course, is done on a fee-for-services basis.

In my experience, arrangements of this kind must be structured carefully to make economic sense. In order to make sure the supplier's contribution is greater than a few key members of management, the supplier must have economies of scale to offer. Often the supplier has not been a supplier in this area previously or, perhaps, has not established itself as a supplier at all. The lack of additional resources, coupled with the shared control, can prevent the supplier from implementing significant process changes.

Often, relationships of this type are predicated on the supplier being able to bring new customers to the joint venture; however, in many instances the supplier is in competition with the joint venture through selling consulting services or creating new joint ventures.

Another problem is the lack of any effective exit strategy for the buyer. If the joint venture does work and manages to create value, the intrinsic value of the company that is created is depressed because the supplier has an effective veto over its sale. This means that the only likely buyer for the entity is the supplier. If a fair buy/sell agreement is not in place from the beginning, the result could be that the buyer would be paid a fraction of its market value, or it would be unable to realize its value at all. It often would be better if all concerned were to focus on the creation of value, based on real and demonstrable leverage that utilizes structures that strengthen accountability and encourage outside investment.

Finally, the intention is that the parties will benefit though profit sharing. However, the lack of leverage makes it difficult for genuine value to be created, and the relationship runs the risk of making paper profits only by adding cost to the services it otherwise would have received from its internal infrastructure. It is not that this type of relationship can never work. But, as always with outsourcing, the participants must be clear about the necessity for adequate leverage if value is to be created; unfortunately, this type of structure tends to obscure these issues. Having said all that, there are some examples of successful outsourcing joint ventures.

• *Supply Chain Management Through Joint Venture.* Outsourcing helped Farmland Industries Inc. reengineer an entire business process and its supply chain network. The huge agricultural co-op accomplished this massive restructuring through a joint venture with Ernst & Young LLP, an outsourcing consulting firm.

The co-op needed a transformation because it lacked access to traditional capital markets due to its co-op structure. (It served 1,400 different organizations.) It also had been using manual spreadsheets and methods of accounting for routing and returning profits to its customers due to the vast number of non-integrated computer systems among the various businesses.

The Ernst & Young team installed and maintains SAP enterprise integration software that they have used successfully to reengineer Farmland's key process (its supply chain management practices). The co-op expects a return on its investment in the joint venture through cutting millions of dollars off fertilizer storage costs, cost savings in its new IT accounting tracking systems, and selling the joint venture's services to other buyers.

• *A Healthy Proposition as Joint Venture.* The use of information-sharing systems is at the heart of why a joint venture was formed between a U.S. telecommunications company, Ameritech Corp., and a U.S. healthcare company, Aurora Health Care. They formed Wisconsin Health Information Network to meet the needs of hospitals, physicians, and other healthcare providers who are customers of this supplier's network. It is such a success that not only do the joint venture partners have profit to split, but the healthcare providers who use its services also save a great deal of money on transactions using this service.

## Summarizing Approaches

In my opinion, a buyer is best served through either the single-source or the best-of-breed outsourcing formats. The alliance concept combines the worst of all worlds. As outsourcing becomes a more widely adopted tool, more companies appear to be adopting the best-of-breed vehicle. I should note that I am addressing situations where the outsourcing services being sought are all in the same general field, such as data processing or logistics. Clearly, where the services desired are very different from one another, multiple suppliers would not come into contact with one another, nor would they compete; so those situations would not be problematic.

## Contractual Structure of the Relationship

As you build your outsourcing relationships, it is necessary to select the most appropriate approach and then move on to a repeatable way of documenting and executing it. Of course, attorneys are always part of the contract process. Their work becomes much more productive, however, if the business people do their work properly first.

As explained earlier, switching costs are extremely high, so it makes little sense for a buyer to frequently change suppliers. A buyer who does so demonstrates that it has not learned how to manage its suppliers. For a supplier, frequent changes mean it constantly either would have to re-compete to win new business or face the prospect of going out of business.

That is why I so strongly recommend long-term relationships with repeated short-term contracts. In the long run, this is best for both parties. Having re-emphasized this basic point, here is my advice in the art of building a sustainable contracting vehicle that provides flexibility for the buyer and produces accountability from the supplier.

***Issues to be Covered in the Contract.*** Historically, most outsourcing contracts have been inflexible and have had a tendency to focus on legal issues to the detriment of business issues. I do not mean to imply that legal issues are unimportant— only that in the production of value they are secondary to business issues. Unfortunately, most outsourcing contracts obscure the most important issues. These issues are:

1. what services are being purchased,
2. how services will be measured,
3. how services will be priced, and
4. how the parties will be held accountable.

Of course, while you must give adequate attention to the more esoteric legal issues, many outsourcing contracts are allowed to evolve into complex, single-purpose instruments that drive substantial cost into the transaction. Not surprisingly, the attorneys have a tendency to take over. Since they are paid to avoid risk, they take their responsibility seriously and dominate the business discussions.

Such complexity makes a contract less useful than it otherwise could be. The great danger of interlacing the terms and conditions with the business issues is that legal arguments tend to take precedence over business issues; they also may overly convolute the contract. This can result in shortchanging the business issues and making poor agreements.

Furthermore, if different services are lumped together in a single legal contract, they can work at cross-purposes. As I have already mentioned, the appropriate duration of contracts may differ in the light of the underlying rate of technological or business change. The appropriate metrics also will differ widely for different kinds of services.

*The Need for a Flexible Contract.* A lack of flexibility is a great danger. One of the benefits of flexibility is that new services can be added, and the buyer can keep rolling on with the same supplier. This is beneficial to both parties. The supplier will not be faced with the prospect of losing all its business at once and will understand that it has ongoing risk. It will tend to view the relationship as an ongoing one, rather than as a win/lose proposition in which all costs are borne at once.

This allows the buyer to receive new types of value and see the supplier as more than a menial servant. It allows the supplier to invest in the relationship with the expectation that its investments will be rewarded when they create value. Of course, it is possible that the supplier is not an expert in every area, but that does not mean the buyer will not want to keep working with a particular supplier. The contract should provide the flexibility and the incentive for the supplier to keep earning its position while avoiding a huge economic setback, like the abrupt loss of tens of million of dollars, should things not work out to perfection.

In a flexible arrangement, both sides are encouraged to work constantly on the relationship—as in a marriage, it's good to bring flowers once in a while. With these mechanisms in place, a basis for a true win-win relationship is established, and the relationship will extend well beyond what otherwise would be its normal life.

Flexibility in an outsourcing contract enables the parties to make changes without having to renegotiate the entire contract and without triggering termination charges. As changes are required, they can be made to the individual services rather than to the overall contract. This also allows for easy additions and subtractions of services with different term lengths, without triggering complete renegotiations.

This is important, as renegotiations can become very contentious and disruptive to the ongoing operations of both organizations. If smaller, rather than larger, changes are made, the overall threat to both organizations is significantly reduced; and the corresponding risk of business disruptions and unneeded hostilities is reduced. This also lessens the threat to the supplier because, in many cases, the number of its contracts that extend into the future is the key to its stock valuation.

An example of the need for flexibility occurred in the Roll-Royce Aerospace Group/EDS alliance. At a strategic level, this alliance has worked very much as was originally anticipated, in that EDS and Rolls-Royce have worked together to redesign the Rolls-Royce process and to replace its IT systems to implement the new process.

However, had the participants not made provision at the outset for flexibility, it would not have been as successful an endeavor. Flexibility has played a vital role, because many changes have become necessary since the outset. The role of EDS was to transform Rolls-Royce's program through BPO. Supplier initiatives included, among other things, lean manufacturing, improving the responsiveness and efficiency of the supply chain, bringing concept to market faster, and then implementing new systems for the new processes. EDS, therefore, took steps to increase quality and productivity.

But world conflicts and national budgets changed the aerospace market. This fact, together with Rolls-Royce's success in its latest commercial engine arena, led to a need to refocus and design initiatives to help Rolls-Royce increase throughput—the ability to make more engines faster.

Flexibility and good working relationships at all levels of the company are absolutely essential. The supplier's work has to be able to change, because sometimes Rolls-Royce is aiming at productivity improvement; sometimes it is aiming at throughput; and, at other times, it is aiming at both. In order for the supplier's compensation to be fair, the participants must have the ability to change the relationship's gain-sharing mechanism; otherwise, they could not maintain an alignment to objectives.

When an entire contract is put at risk because of a minor change, the supplier is put in a tight position in which it feels its back is to the wall and it has no alternative but to adopt an aggressive position. This, in turn, causes the buyer to adopt an equally aggressive position, leading to a negative spiral. At best, this affects the ongoing relationship; at worst, it results in a separation that does not benefit either party.

The alternative is a reasonable compromise. I am constantly astounded by the positions taken in contract renegotiations when, in other contexts, I have seen both parties willing to accept a compromise or even the other party's position.

***The Length of the Contract.*** Nothing is more certain than change, and the best outsourcing contracts recognize this. Like solid prenuptial agreements, successful outsourcing contracts have the built-in flexibility to recognize and act on the fluid nature of change. While the newer style contracts are short term, they recognize long-term relationships between the parties.

Short-term contracts are preferable for several reasons. First, no one can predict technology and business conditions for more than three years in advance, thus making contracts increasingly outdated as time progresses. Second, short-term contracts motivate supplier performance because suppliers realize the buyers may switch suppliers when the contract expires. Finally, short-term contracts allow companies to recover and learn more quickly from mistakes.

**Master Procurement Vehicle**

The following is a contractual framework, which can be utilized in any type of outsourcing relationship. It separates the legal terms and conditions from the business issues. It also allows for multiple types of services to exist under the same contracting vehicle, even though they may have different natural contract terms and business conditions. This approach allows both parties to focus on the important business issues without overly intermingling the legal and contractual issues.

# Outsourcing Relationship Structure

In the agreement depicted in the diagram, the supplier will attach language regarding specific services to be provided. For example, it may indicate that it will provide data processing, payroll, accounting, administration or procurement services. (Most suppliers confine themselves to specific niche areas, although some offer multiple outsourcing systems. Norell Software, Inc., for instance, offers recruiting, office cleaning, reprographics, and other administrative functions.)

The procurement vehicle establishes the standard clauses within which the supplier would be comfortable operating. These clauses must be fair; they are not to be a means by which the buyer gains an unfair advantage over the supplier.

It is best to come to the negotiating table with a well thought-out and generally fair contract. Service agreements should be attached to it. Term lengths must be appropriate for the service being offered. For example, in an environment with a high velocity of change (such as desktop or telecommunications), a two-year or three-year relationship is appropriate. In an environment slower to change (such as payroll), a longer relationship can be effective. In a truly stable environment (such as facilities administration), five years may be the best contract length.

So make the punishment fit the crime—match the term to the rate of technology change and the conditions associated with that business or service.

Each service must have adequate descriptions defining what the supplier will provide, along with appropriate boundaries and with the proper service levels (metrics) associated with the provided service. In order to avoid confusion, the contract should define and measure the results of the services to be provided, rather than weave these differing elements into a master agreement. This makes it easy for management to see what it is buying; how to measure the results; how to ensure service at a fair price; and how to make the term equal to the reasonable life of the service.

This model contract has a place for value agreements based on business-oriented metrics, allowing one to introduce shorter-term initiatives with their associated compensation and rewards. In a monolithic contract, rewards tend to be spread out over the length of the contract; in this model, they can be more appropriately aligned with value.

This contract is also designed to prevent the shift of control in the supplier's favor. By contrast, in a long-term contract, where the buyer may pay more, the supplier's objectives end up dominating the contract. On the plus side, the supplier confronts less risk in the short term. It will not be put in a position where it could lose all its business at once; and it will have a happier customer because the relationship will be kept in alignment with the buyer's business objectives.

There is also the potential for continued growth because this master procurement vehicle allows buyers to add new services. By structuring the agreement so the supplier has to unbundle its pricing, the contract encourages alignment of expectations between those managers who manage primarily through the impact on their budgets. This promotes clear lines of communication between the parties.

Admittedly, the supplier may resist the shortening of its agreements because its stock valuation is driven by business backlog. By not signing a long-term contract, a buyer, in effect, reduces that backlog. Although the supplier probably will get the business, that fact is not guaranteed. Friction between the two parties may arise over this; even so, there is no excuse for a buyer to accede to a process that will guarantee it an unfavorable result. To a buyer that finds itself in this situation, I say "stick by your guns." In a changing world, backlog is an illusion anyway, and financial analysts ought to learn that fact.

# Chapter 10

# THE PHILOSOPHER'S STONE

*"Even Moses got excited when he saw the promised land."*
— Lyle Lovett, country-western singer

The medieval alchemists sought to combine different substances and discover a secret balance that would have the transformative power of turning ordinary minerals into gold. Like them, you may be searching for that secret formula. Maybe you are an executive seeking new ways to make your company competitive. Or you may be a corporate version of Alexander the Great in pursuit of new worlds to conquer. In either case, you probably will dabble within this new, 21st-century form of alchemy.

As an experienced alchemist, I have strived to lay bare outsourcing's principles and guide you through some of its potential snares. This is not a spell book about a mysterious process that may or may not work. It is a book of principles and insights gained through the construction and management of many successful outsourcing relationships.

Like the alchemists of old, you will find that practicing this art is neither easy nor free of risk. Where the alchemists had poisons and inquisitions to worry about, you will face resistance from those whom outsourcing affects and the disapproval of those who do not understand its value. However, the value is real, and the process is tried and true. If you heed the advice this book offers and employ the principles successfully, you can be part of the value-creation practice known as outsourcing.

Good luck, and may you prosper greatly by it!

# APPENDICES ON
# ADDITIONAL RESOURCES

*"Knowledge is not enough; we must apply."*
—Goethe

Now that you've read the book and you are armed with knowledge and insights about how outsourcing works successfully, you may be like Alice in Lewis Carroll's *Alice in Wonderland*, who asked the Cheshire Cat: "Would you tell me, please, which way I ought to go from here?" The Cat, you'll recall, replied with "That depends a good deal on where you want to get to."

I have provided these appendices as additional resources to guide you further down the path of turning lead into gold through outsourcing.

For supplementary and ongoing insights, you'll want to check out Appendix A. If you're ready to take the next step and procure outsourcing for one or more of your company's business processes or functions, you'll be excited about the information in Appendix B.

f you need to conduct an assessment or feasibil-y study to aid in your company's decision to out-source, you'll find the information in Appendix C helpful.

Appendix D provides guidelines for transitioning a buyer's work to the supplier's environment. Finally, Appendix E will help a buyer establish a governance plan whereby it will be able to manage the out-sourcing relationship on an ongoing basis.

# Appendix A

*The Outsourcing Center*
*www.outsourcing-center.com*

The Outsourcing Center is the global leader in providing insights into outsourcing. The Center's research site, search engines and supplier database are popular features, and hundreds of buyers and suppliers have their questions answered daily by our outsourcing experts and analysts. The Outsourcing Center dominates the industry with a wealth of authoritative, insightful information. The site's visitors make it the largest Web outsourcing community in the world.

Its related Web sites provide comprehensive information also in these areas: academics, analysis, Australia, backoffice, benchmarking, benefits, business-to-business, desktop, eCommerce, Europe, finance and accounting, government, healthcare, HR, international, legal, logistics, networks, offshore, service level agreements, supply chain management and transition management.

The Center publishes the *Outsourcing Journal* (www.outsourcing-journal.com), a monthly online journal featuring case study articles that highlight successful outsourcing relationships, as well as current trends, strategies and analysis. Each topic is presented from three distinct perspectives: the customer, the supplier, and the analyst. Back issues are archived for easy online access.

The Center also oversees the ASP Outsourcing Center and the BPO Outsourcing Center (along with the associated *ASP OutsourcingJournal* and *BPO OutsourcingJournal*). (URLS to these sites are: www.asp-outsourcing-center.com, www.asp-out-sourcing-journal.com, www.bpo-outsourcing-center.com, and www.bpo-outsourcing-journal.com.)

# Appendix B

## The Outsourcing Exchange
## www.outsourcing-exchangecenter.com

As CEO, I decided to use the Outsourcing Center as the means of curing outsourcing's weakest spot. You probably realize the weak spot if you've read this far into this book—it's the procurement phase. That is the most crucial time for establishing foundations for success in outsourcing. Unfortunately, it's also where the most dangerous pitfalls for buyers reside. So we at the Outsourcing Center set about changing the way outsourcing is procured in the 21st century. We've removed the hazards!

Let me tell you about a better way to buy outsourcing and, more importantly, the effect it will have on the industry.

As established earlier, success in an outsourcing relationship is determined up-front, during the procurement phase. That important process is far more than determining which supplier's bid is the best price. The only way a buyer can actually get the results it wants to buy is to establish those facts before it goes to market with a request for a bid on its work.

Historically, the buyers who have understood the importance of the procurement phase have had two costly options—incurring the significant expense of a consultant to guide them through the process, or attempting to handle it on their own. The companies who opted to handle it on their own frequently have ended up making extremely costly errors and creating relationships that often failed. As I explained in earlier chapters, this is because buyers lack outsourcing knowledge that would put them on a level playing ground with the suppliers with whom they must try to negotiate a fair deal.

So we at the Outsourcing Center leveraged our expertise along with the Internet's technological advancements and economies of scale, and we created the Outsourcing Exchange Center. The Exchange is a unique business-to-business e-marketplace that delivers unprecedented opportunities for win/win outsourcing relationships for both buyers and suppliers because its methodology and tools are based on the proven, successful principles explained in this book.

### Tools That Ensure Success

The Outsourcing Exchange Center gives buyers—at no cost—all the tools necessary to submit and conduct a bid (through the Exchange), negotiate the contract and price, and award the work to the chosen supplier. It also features online videos that enhance the instructions and techniques.

The challenges of procurement are the need to put the outsourcing agreement in place more quickly and to eliminate the high costs. Before the

Outsourcing Exchange Center, procurement could cost hundreds of thousands of dollars—even a million or more—and take as long as nine months to a year and a half to complete the transactions. With the Exchange, the procurement is reduced to two weeks to a month, and the transaction costs are drastically lower for both buyers and suppliers.

In each Exchange Package are several tools, including documents that, once customized to a buyer's unique situation and requirements, are put together to form the online Bid Document. These include:

- Service descriptions (the description of the scope and boundaries of the services the supplier is expected to deliver);
- Service levels (descriptions of the service levels at which the supplier is expected to perform);
- Metrics (the measurements and intervals by which the supplier's performance will be monitored);
- Contract (a balanced document with standard terms and conditions, which is also flexible enough to withstand the inevitable changes that will occur in technology and in the buyer's marketplace during the length of a contract);
- Pricing structure mechanisms;
- A transition plan module (the plan for moving the buyer's work to the supplier's environment in a timely and efficient manner); and
- A governance plan module (the plan by which ongoing relationship will be managed and problems will be resolved).

The Outsourcing Exchange Center gives buyers a significant competitive advantage because they can use the tools described above with the information already prepared and designed for success. The descriptions and metrics are based on industry best practices from prior outsourcing relationships. Through the Outsourcing Exchange Center, the crucial steps in building an effective foundation are already done and are ready for customization to fit the buyer's particular situation.

## Ensuring Market Competition

Suppliers also benefit from the tools at the Exchange. In addition to the clear, effective service descriptions, service levels and metrics, suppliers use the Exchange's simplified response mechanisms for their bids. The streamlined process reduces transaction costs for suppliers, thus enabling them to bid a greater number of deals and also on smaller deals.

This is an important benefit to buyers because, as explained in earlier chapters, the effect of market competition is vital to receiving fair bids from potential suppliers. By using the Exchange, buyers are assured that market forces will prevail until the moment the contractual agreement is actually signed.

At the Exchange, buyers can select potential bidders from the world's most comprehensive outsourcing supplier database. Buyers search the database by using such parameters as geographic areas, industry, outsourced process areas and certification. Suppliers have the added-value advantage of distinguishing their company's offerings and capabilities by opting for the Exchange's certification process. This is a another win/win benefit, as it also helps buyers in their process of qualifying the suppliers invited to respond to the Bid Document.

## Conducting the Bid Process Through the Exchange

The Exchange Package includes worksheets and instructions that help buyers evaluate suppliers' bids on an apples-to-apples basis and also to understand negotiation strategies.

At the Exchange, buyers have three options once the suppliers' bids have been submitted. A buyer may simply choose a supplier from the submitted bids, or it can decide to enter into due diligence and/or online negotiations with some or all of the bidding suppliers. If it happens that the buyer is not pleased with any of the bids, it can conduct a reverse auction in an effort to drive the price lower. (In such an event, the buyer would need to ensure that the new, lower bids are for the same scope and level of services as the prior bids.)

Sometimes suppliers' responses to a Bid Document raise new issues; consequently, it's often wise for buyers to conduct due diligence or negotiations. For these purposes, the Exchange includes private, secure communications vehicles for conducting negotiations online.

Buyers also may decide to downselect bidding

suppliers—eliminating all but two or three—and then ask for a resubmitted bid reflecting negotiations that may have taken place. This ensures market competition forces until the contract is actually signed.

Once the winning supplier is selected, buyers are ready to implement the transition plan and governance team and transition their work to the supplier's environment.

An added value and extremely beneficial feature of the Exchange is the additional assistance available on an as-needed basis. At any time throughout the procurement process, a buyer may request remote or onsite help from outsourcing consultants or the Exchange's legal partner.

## Pitfalls Eliminated at the Exchange

At the Outsourcing Exchange Center, we have built sturdy bridges over the precarious chasms into which buyers usually fall. We eliminate the suppliers' power to use marketing techniques that influence buyers to buy something they don't need. By providing buyers with documents that have pre-designed service descriptions, service levels and metrics based on industry best practices and benchmarks, they have the documents that clearly state to the suppliers the desired outcome and results that the buyer wants to purchase. The Exchange helps with the disintermediation between buyers and suppliers and increases the overall quality of an outsourcing agreement for long-term success.

## Standing on Standards

I'm sure you remember from Chapter 3 that outsourcing's first pioneer was Ross Perot. Part of his economic success was built on the practice of standardization. He was able to create great economies of scale by providing offerings that were focused on regulated industries with similar operations and procedures.

The same principle is in effect at the Outsourcing Exchange Center. Although the documents and tools in the Exchange Packages are designed for buyers to customize, their starting points are based on industry standardized service descriptions, service levels and metrics, and contracts.

More importantly, we're taking standardization to its ultimate best use. The masses of buyers and suppliers around the world who use the Outsourcing Exchange Center are exposed to its best practices and benchmarks that will then become the standards in quality for outsourcing agreements. Moreover, we are transforming outsourcing procurement itself—from an outdated, costly and very lengthy process—to a streamlined, online process that reduces transaction time and costs while it enhances quality. I believe the Exchange's methodology will become the industry standard for buying outsourcing. It will be the ultimate win for buyers and suppliers alike.

You'll find the Exchange at www.outsourcing-exchangecenter.com.

# Appendix C

*Conducting a Feasibility Study
for Outsourcing*

The first step in assessing whether a company should outsource one (or more) of its business processes or functions is to conduct an initial review of the company's business objectives for outsourcing. This will help to define the scope of the project.

It will also assist in the buyer's evaluation of the suppliers' bid prices. Let's say, for example, that a buyer wants to provide a cafeteria as part of the benefits package for its employees, but it does not currently have an existing cafeteria environment. So the company decides to outsource the food services functions, together with maintenance of the equipment. Its primary objective is to decrease the amount of time it would take to build and outfit a cafeteria space and hire experts. Its second objective is to eliminate the cost of regulatory licenses and an in-house employee to maintain and update that information. Since the cafeteria is to be an employee benefit, another objective will be to ensure employee satisfaction with the food. These three objectives may drive the supplier's price higher, but the buyer will achieve the desired results.

As another example, if the buyer's objective is to obtain state-of-the-art software and hardware and eliminate its maintenance, support and upgrade costs; then the supplier's capability is perhaps even more important than its bid price. In this situation, the buyer also would want to consider estimates of its in-house costs to purchase equipment, maintenance and upgrades. If the objective, on the other hand, is simply to reduce or contain costs, the importance of the supplier's bid price is evident. A list of the most common objectives, or reasons for outsourcing, is included in Chapter 2.

### In-house Baselines

Before a buyer begins the procurement process, it will want to develop in-house baselines against which the supplier's performance results can be quantitatively measured. Typically, an outsourcing relationship will focus on two general baselines: cost and performance.

A cost baseline for a buyer's current in-house process (if it exists) is based on actual invoices paid for each of the components of the in-house process. If the process being considered for outsourcing does not currently exist in the buyer's company, it would need to establish a set of budget parameters and then use estimates for the cost model.

In the outsourced food services example above, the company would want to estimate its costs for new equipment (and maintenance), food and supplies (plus break-out of cost per meal), compensation and benefits for labor (and costs to recruit these new employees, plus management), space (including cleaning and maintenance) and regulatory license fees.

For a process involving IT, for example, the buyer will want to list the costs for hardware, software, licenses, maintenance, tools, data center operation (including, power, air conditioning, supplies), help desk and support, managers and supervisors, etc. The company also will need to determine if it would like the supplier whose bid it selects to assume any of the buyer's current hardware and/or software.

Next, the buyer needs to establish the level of performance it has already achieved in-house. If the service levels it determines for the supplier are a higher level of performance than has been achieved in-house, the buyer must take into consideration that it is increasing the supplier's costs (and the buyer's price).

**Personnel Issues**

Internal issues should also be addressed during the assessment. These include (but are not limited to) political issues and personnel issues. Regarding personnel, the following items need to be considered:

- who (if anyone) will be transferred to the supplier's company;
- who (if anyone) will be retained to manage the contract on an ongoing basis;
- who (if anyone) will be transferred to other positions within the buyer's company;

- who (if anyone) will need to seek other employment and what (if any) severance package will be given to those individuals; and
- pensions.

### "Hidden" Costs

Finally, a buyer also will want to add in the "hidden" costs, such as:

- procurement;
- transitioning to the supplier's environment;
- governance; and
- "switching" costs for early termination (if that unfortunately should happen).

# Appendix D

*Transitioning the Buyer's Work
to the Supplier's Environment*

The transition phase of an outsourcing agreement begins with the transfer of the outsourced processes and activities as of a particular date. It ends with the supplier providing services as described in the contract (including any changes to staff, tools, or processes required to meet the negotiated services and service levels).

To avoid the supplier incurring substantial additional costs and the buyer thus losing confidence in the relationship, a smooth transition is the goal. In order to ensure that it's smooth, it must be planned ahead of time and should be made a part of the contract. In this way, the supplier can be held responsible for its performance in accordance with the plan. The transition plan will look similar to a Service Level Agreement, in that it should include a service description, service level and metrics.

In addition to determining the timing and method of transfer of personnel, hardware, software licenses, supplier interface formats and mechanisms, the transition plan should contain the following elements:

- Development of back-filling plans regarding personnel;

- Preparation of announcements to personnel; and
- Negotiation of personnel policies and practices.

Also included in the transition plan should be the following administrative items:

- Establishment of communication methods;
- Decisions regarding invoice processing, timing, format and backup;
- Establishment of a change management and authorization process;
- Definition of new service categories and an implementation process;
- Refinement of service level reporting; and
- Definition of report structure, timing and monitoring.

# Appendix E

*Governance: Managing the
Ongoing Relationship*

The governance team is the key management interface between the buyer's business units and the supplier. The creation and empowerment of this governance team is critical to the ongoing management of the relationship.

The governance team will consist of a small group from both the supplier's and the buyer's companies. The members of the group should be empowered senior executives and/or senior managers who can make binding decisions regarding the outsourcing relationship. The group will have both proactive and reactive responsibilities.

Proactively, the governance team will:

- create alignment between the supplier, the governance team and the buyer's business units;
- help with creating or modifying business processes needed to manage the relationship;
- lower the cost of managing the relationship;
- ensure that the supplier complies with the contract and delivers the desired contribution;
- provide methodology for calculating the value of the relationship; and

- reduce or eliminate in-scope/out-of-scope discussions.

Reactively, the governance team will:
- revise the roles and responsibilities of the buyer as needed;
- revise the roles and responsibilities of the supplier as needed;
- revise the performance reporting process;
- establish more precise definitions of scope, services and business process interfaces;
- establish effective measurements, penalties and, if appropriate, incentives;
- train the governance team and senior management in how to manage a supplier in order to gain expected results; and
- serve as an arbiter in issue resolution.

Governance team members should be trained in their duties. Stepping into this important role unprepared will create problems for the relationship and will hinder the supplier's delivery of high-quality services. Each team member needs to develop skills in contract interpretation, creative problem solving and strategic planning in order to effectively control the supplier and meet the buyer's business needs.

# ABOUT THE AUTHOR

Peter Bendor-Samuel is the CEO of the Outsourcing Center, which offers the *Outsourcing Journal*—an international, on-line magazine dedicated to the outsourcing industry. The Outsourcing Center tracks the growth of outsourcing throughout the world and presents monthly information on a broad spectrum of issues. As editor of this premier on-line magazine, Bendor-Samuel is the driving force behind the Outsourcing Center's rapid growth, as outsourcing integrates within virtually every function of modern global enterprise.

Bendor-Samuel is also the president and founder of the Everest Group, the consulting division of the Outsourcing Center. Everest specializes in helping major companies and government entities worldwide with outsourcing management techniques. The Everest Group has played a vital role in ensuring the success of major international outsourcing contracts, within the U.S. and abroad, which, in total, are valued in billions of dollars. Bendor-Samuel is widely recognized as a leading global authority on outsourcing. His expertise at identifying trends in the workplace and creating innovative outsourcing models is in high demand. He has helped many organizations save substantial costs by outsourcing various business functions.

As a former executive at EDS, he worked on more than 100 outsourcing engagements, and in the process, fine-tuned his broad understanding of the important components in outsourcing. Understanding both sides of the outsourcing relationship makes him the ultimate expert on the outsourcing industry. He passionately and effectively communicates the "big picture" through his many articles and in *Turning Lead Into Gold*. His expertise creates a constant demand for speaking engagements at many conferences and corporate events throughout the world.

Japan's Prime Minister honored Bendor-Samuel with the title "The Honorable Advisor to the Strategic Outsourcing Council." He has a BBA and a MBA from Baylor University with disciplines in economics, computer science, and management.

For more information on the Outsourcing Center, please visit: http://www.outsourcingexchangecenter.com.

# Excellence
PUBLISHING

Since 1984, *Executive Excellence* has provided business leaders and managers with the best and latest thinking on leadership development, managerial effectiveness, and organizational productivity. Each issue is filled with insights and answers from top business executives, trainers, and consultants—information you won't find in any other publication.

**For more information** please call
Executive Excellence Publishing at:

## 1-800-304-9782
or visit our Web site: **www.eep.com**